Lewis Wingfield

Barbara Philpot

A Study of Manners and Morals (1727 to 1737.): Vol. II.

Lewis Wingfield

Barbara Philpot
A Study of Manners and Morals (1727 to 1737.): Vol. II.

ISBN/EAN: 9783337266745

Printed in Europe, USA, Canada, Australia, Japan

Cover: Foto ©ninafisch / pixelio.de

More available books at **www.hansebooks.com**

A Study of Manners and Morals.

(1727 TO 1737.)

BY THE
HON. LEWIS WINGFIELD,
AUTHOR OF
'LADY GRIZEL,' 'ABIGEL ROWE,' 'IN HER MAJESTY'S KEEPING,'
ETC.

IN THREE VOLUMES.
VOL. II.

LONDON:
RICHARD BENTLEY AND SON,
Publishers in Ordinary to Her Majesty the Queen.
1885.
[*All Rights Reserved.*]

CONTENTS OF VOL. II.

CHAPTER		PAGE
I. NEUTRAL GROUND		1
II. A RISE IN THE WORLD		37
III. 'EXCISE'		73
IV. A THIEVES' HOLIDAY		116
V. WORRIES		151
VI. 'TILTING AT WINDMILLS'		191
VII. 'ECLIPSE'		223
VIII. 'SPORT'.		246
IX. 'MRS. BELFIELD GROWS MORE PERPLEXED'		268
X. 'PITFALLS'		288

BARBARA PHILPOT.

CHAPTER I.

NEUTRAL GROUND.

THE Duchess of Queensberry's hurricanes were unique, and when she opened the spacious saloons of her town residence, as mixed an assembly answered the call as the collection gathered by Noah.

Although the Court never forgave the affair of the 'Beggar's Opera,' the Duchess lost favour in so honourable a way that her ostracism came to be regarded as a formal matter; which was fortunate, since she looked on the country as a field for martyrs, and speedily grew tired of playing backgammon with the chaplain.

Her parties, whether earthquakes or hurricanes, were so splendid that everyone below the rank of royalty considered themselves aggrieved if omitted from the list. And so her drawing-rooms became a neutral ground on which combatants could meet and parley as under a flag of truce.

Even Mrs. Belfield and Mr. Medlicote, members of the Household, were carried sometimes from St. James's to Burlington Gardens, and the following day, at the Queen's rising, both she and the King would be fiercely curious to know what had passed; who had been present, and what had been said, putting endless questions till the narrators were fairly exhausted.

Her Grace, on the principle of diamond cut diamond, rather enjoyed the polyglot nature of the entertainments. She cultivated persons of extremely opposite views. For years she and Swift kept up an intimate and sparkling correspondence, although in this world they never met.

The Dawley farmer emerged at her bidding from his hermitage. The only Tory of eminence whom she eschewed was Pope. But then, 'twas agreed that that backbiter was a shade too crabbed for ordinary mortals; that he could never find a visitor unless he hired him with a bottle of right Burgundy, and that 'twas best to leave so cantankerous a snarler to stew in his own venom.

Good-natured Walpole set the fashion to the Whigs. It amused him to indulge in playful passages of arms with Pulteney, Chesterfield and Co.; to gibe at Mr. Gay, who, most easy-going of versifiers assumed pinched airs in the presence of the Minister.

'I am quite happy,' her Grace's tame cat would say demurely, when slily rated by Sir Robert; 'seek no acquaintance, and court no favours. For sauce to my meat enjoy a wholesome hatred of the outer world.'

To which Sir Robert would reply with his great laugh:

'Giddy idler! But for her Grace's teasing you'd die of inactivity! A coach-and-six, with a Blenheim spaniel for company, is your utmost exercise, varied by a tiff about bread-and-butter!'

And then Mr. Gay would retort, being as fond as a wench of the last word:

'Sure, parliaments and kingdoms quarrel for no better cause!'

My Lady Suffolk, stout, deaf, and stupid, could rouse herself to shake off for an hour the yoke of royal tyranny. Not that her presence enlivened the scene, for the post of mistress *en titre* became more gruesome daily by reason of the King's quarrels with his son; and her dull wits appeared to grow more blunt.

My Lady Suffolk liked Mr. Gay, smart, fluttering may-fly, for his powers were not above her own intellectual level. In his interest she deplored her lack of influence, for was not his 'Trivia' vastly entertaining with its doggrel descriptions of boots, gutters, spatterdashes—details under her nose daily, which she could see, and smell, and appreciate? How cosy it was, too, to squat by his side at supper and gibe at Walpole, while he helped her to titbits. She was, in her groping way, afraid of Walpole, suspecting that, as Caroline's staunch friend, he wished to oust her from the post of slave, to which she clung with fawning tenacity.

Sir Robert and Mr. Medlicote agreed on the subject of her Grace's gatherings. Court-life was so monstrous dull, the chatter in the King's presence so insipid and monotonous, that Ranulph often vowed that but for the gossip picked up at the Duchess's his faculties would mildew. The scandal of the coffee-houses was woefully insufficient. In the Queen's closet 'twas otherwise, for there the talk was of books, of recondite religious speculation, of pictures; varied by verbal conflicts with Mrs. Belfield which kept the air wholesome and breezy.

The Honourable Pamela and he suited each other exactly, he thought. Her smart talk, seething with the recriminative zest of a good deal of lemon, made, he declared, the prettiest refreshing sherbet. He saw no objection to the extreme sharpness of her tongue.

'The object of a young woman's existence,' he argued, 'was to pique the men, to sharpen their wits by plaguing;' and in this art Mrs. Belfield was proficient.

Despite her want of beauty, there was a distinguished air of breeding about the Queen's bedchamber-woman, and a facility of retort and repartee which caused her, although secretly disliked, to shine in society; while her excessive worldliness was a tacit guarantee that, well married, she would know better than to go wrong, however loose her behaviour with the sparks might appear to be.

It occurred to Medlicote that some day in the dim future he might do worse than give his name to Pamela; that she would look vastly well at the end of a table (in private, of course, they would not meet), and that, no longer reduced to petty scheming by poverty, she would do credit as a modish wife.

Thus it will be perceived that one, at least, of the astute damsel's plans seemed likely to succeed, should she warmly go in for a Beatrice and Benedick wooing.

Looking among the maids of honour and daughters of polite houses, Ranulph could see none who would suit him better, or as well; for, indeed, the female quality cared little at this time what was thought of 'em, and worldly prudence took the place of a higher virtue.

But the Honourable Pamela, whilst pleased by her progress with Ranulph, had no notion of so foolishly committing herself. As things were turning out, it was by no means clear that King George's Vice-Chamberlain was a good match for a well-born lady who aspired to enjoy life. There was still no sign of his aspiring to the necessary coronet; while as for his wealth, should the other side triumph in the end he might be proscribed and shorn of his gilding. And others as well as Pamela were veering to the opinion that the wheel would not go round with a swift turn.

Since his arrival from abroad, she and her parent had discussed matters, and she had succeeded, by the gravity of her discourse, in weaning him for a moment from his tailors. He was an odd mixture, was my Lord Belvedere. Clever and quick-sighted when needful, as services abroad had testified, he chose to assume extreme foppishness, and to pretend to care only for dress. Her papa had never been of much use to Mrs. Belfield; and she was annoyed to find that, old and battered, he aped the follies of extreme youth (which was ridiculous, and therefore unseemly), and resented a grown-up daughter. In intervals of cursing his perukier, he hearkened to what she had to say anent the Jacobites, and was by no means sure, all things weighed, that she was wrong.

'Stap my vitals, sirrah!' he grumbled; 'don't you know that a man's wig should, like a woman's mask, show nothing but the eyes?'

''Tis right enough, my lord!' impatiently cried sharp Pamela. 'I see nothing but your nose!'

'Odsblews!' returned my lord, in wrath. 'What care I if my side-face be in eclipse, if my cheeks are like a trumpeter's?'

'If you're a full moon, 'tis your father's fault rather than the wig-maker's,' retorted the undutiful child. "'Tis big and thick enough to keep you warm as you drive down to Dawley.'

To Dawley! Precipitate woman! Commit himself so rashly, the diplomate would not. He had come home intent on a comfortable place about the Court; and, urged by Pamela, was ready to wait awhile, and watch events.

Walpole, to a cautious spectator, seemed intent on suicide. In face of gathering thunderclouds he set his teeth, resolved with Excise to perish, and drag down his friends in his fall.

' 'Twas obstinate madness, nothing else,' asserted Lord Belvedere.

'Twas reported that when the subject came up for debate, the people would come down in their thousands to beard the Minister, and terrify the members by menace into voting against the Bill. Besiege the doors of St. Stephen's! Such a thing had not been done since Orange William saved us from the Pope. Must the man not be mad to despise the public voice, so loudly shouting?

Events to the diplomatist appeared most ominous. Sir Robert Walpole, obstinate as a mule, brought out the Horse and Foot Guards to keep order; but would not give up his Bill. Constables, justices of peace, and magistrates were bidden to curb rioting, while he coerced the country. And, true to their word, the mob surged down, and evilly entreated members, and made a scandal wherein bloodshed was happily averted, no thanks to him. Yet he persisted! The situation was most grave. The *Craftsman* poured forth, like a malignant chorus, its scurrilous reams, which were devoured by the populace. The battle would be fierce and hot. The Dawley clique might triumph; but till they did, 'twould not do to go to Dawley. No. Lord Belvedere would show himself at her Grace of Queensberry's hurricane. Something might be learnt there. Bolingbroke would be present, and Walpole also. He would pay his court to both, and feel his way, keeping a cunning balance.

Of course the throng in Burlington Gardens were full of the scene at the theatre—of the uproar occasioned by the brazen hussy appearing in the unpopular colours—of the assurance with which she had turned the tables by presence of mind and force of character. That such a scene should have occurred in the very presence of the Queen was full of sinister portent.

Bolingbroke was so enchanted that he blazed forth as in the old days, a sparkling, brilliant coruscation, and was as courted as if in favour. Lord Forfar listened with his sad, appreciative smile to the glittering periods of his friend. The mischievous Duchess, tapping Sir Robert with her fan—he found himself quite deserted—whispered:

'What think you now of your arch-enemy? Confess, doth he not shine?'

Sir Robert merely shrugged his shoulders, and took a pinch from her Grace's gala diamond box, remarking, with imperturbable good-humour:

'Shine? Yea, that doth he—like putrefaction in the dark!'

Lord Chesterfield was there, cynical and polished, observing to her Grace through his thin lips that Sir Robert was as coarse as a bargeman; to which the Duchess retorted that my Lord Chesterfield would hate him more deeply who should say that he was awkward, or ill-bred, than one who dubbed him 'rogue.'

'I must confess,' returned his lordship, 'that I do not like to see gentlemen imitate their servants. You observe young men of a morning in dirty blue frocks and boots—in London—with hair greasy and unpowdered, and great oaken sticks, who are at once the support and terror, and the victims of the lowest tippling-houses. Manners are dying out. I know of but one exception—my Lord Bolingbroke.'

'Twas a splendid party. Hundreds of wax-lights illumined the silken walls. The floors were gracefully picked out with a design of fruit and flowers in coloured chalks. Glow-worm lamps depended from the trees in the garden.

My Lord Belvedere—a gorgeous figure, as parrot-hued as Bolingbroke himself—was elbowing through the perspiring crowd, and took the earliest opportunity of narrowly scanning the Minister. He was strong—no doubt he was strong—stood firmly on his sturdy limbs. T'other was sparkling—dazzling; but there was not the sense of conscious immovable strength so conspicuous about Sir Robert. Pamela must be wrong; so was this buzzing cloud of wiseacres. She must be in love with the Scotch malcontent—no doubt of it; and love, as usual, was blinding her feminine tact. That his own flesh and blood should not be more sensible! He, my Lord Belvedere, was not in love—not he; and would act warily for both.

'How few,' he mused, with dissatisfaction, 'know how to love and how to hate!'

The diplomatist knew love to be a madness, very often fatal to the beloved one; he knew that open hate is a rash violence, fatal usually to the hater. He nourished nor love nor hate either for Walpole or for Bolingbroke, for George or James; but cultivated an ardent and far-seeing affection—for himself.

Gazing now with experienced ken, he perceived Walpole to be quiet and resolute. And yet—was it not possible that a seeming certainty of ultimate triumph was mere dogged obstinacy? Like Pamela, her parent ardently desired to lift a corner of the veil and peep. Caution became his years and experience. A middle course must be maintained. Such a situation of tension as this present one could not last. Feathers would soon show the direction of the wind; and one so keen of sight as our diplomatist, through the furze-bush of his exaggerated periwig, would detect the earliest indications. He therefore lapsed into his most languid and lackadaisical manner, seeming to find the labour of standing more than could be borne; ogled the ladies through his quizzing-glasses, dropping to right and left a lively compliment, whilst offering his case of sweetmeats.

'The British climate agrees, I hope, with my Lord Belvedere?' remarked Sir Robert. 'Nay, nay! No sugar-plums for me! Spiced ale and a toast is more in my way. That rose-tinted velvet of yours on a silver ground should kill some of 'em with envy. A plain fellow like me, you see, finds cinnamon-cloth answer every purpose!'

'With a blue ribbon meandering upon it, stap me! and a star of brilliants!' returned my lord, shaking back his ruffles of Venice point with a graceful wave. 'The ladies are kind enough to allow me a fertile genius for dress; but, rat me, 'tis fatiguing! Those coxcombs, the fop-makers, besieged me this morning for the pattern of my French dog-ear surtout, and gave me no peace till they had it—strike me speechless!'

'Since your return you've devoted yourself to London gaieties?'

'Egad, you're right, Sir Robert! My life's an

eternal round of delights from ten, when I get up—
'tis the worst thing in the world for the complexion
to rise sooner—until I go to rest. What with the
Park and the chocolate-house and the play, and a
hand at quadrille or ombre, and an intrigue or two
with some lady of quality——'

'Fie!' cried her Grace in passing. 'You sad
man! Now that you are back, we poor women must
be careful.'

'Can your ladyship find me tolerable?' asked his
lordship, with a low bow and a grin to show his false
teeth. 'I feel cursedly like a stage-player of a
morning. In the glare of your thousand candles
you are safe and we disarmed—mere blinking owls!
In the dusk I warrant you I'll be in danger. Why
did Daphne fly from Apollo but because he wore
daylight wreathed about his brows?'

A murmur of approval greeted his lordship's sally.

Lord Chesterfield was quite comforted, for the
manner of the new comer showed the best breeding.
Lord Belvedere deprecated his daughter's sharp
tongue, aware that wit, while it dazzles, also
scorches, and that to talk genteelly about nothing
is a necessary art to a courtier. Indeed, he had
lectured her, somewhat late in the day, about her
abrupt method and speech.

'An offended fool,' he had sagely said, 'or an
affronted page of the backstairs may injure you more
than the praise of ten geniuses can remedy.'

Whereupon the naughty damsel had perked her chin and roundly bidden him to leave off doting, and march into t'other world rather than assume the pedagogue.

'Mr. Gay,' he cried, 'stap me, but you are a nauseous rascal! What a halcyon life is yours to our humdrum existence; fed upon orange-water squeezed by the loveliest hand; sprinkled with rose-essence; buried by her Grace to the chin in burrage, balm and burnet—you luxurious sybarite! Why is Fortune so partial in her dispensations? And how blessed is she, recognised in the flesh as goddess of the arts, with her own poet at all hours ready to tune an inspired lyre—adored by the men, envied by the women, feminine acme of happiness. What privileges belong to our dear Duchess! She makes uneasy the whole creation; gathers around her all that is brilliant and refined and learned, making each shine out his best. I vow a library always makes me sad, for there the best authors are as much squeezed as a porter at the Coronation; while here, they bask in crowds in the rays of the noonday sun, exhaling themselves in praise.'

'Twas vastly pretty—the smallest of small-talk, like a flinging of light sixpences, which circulate freely.

Seduced by *les bienséances*, you forgot that this elegant gentleman was half a doll, painted, stuffed, and perfumed, and had one leg in the grave; so true is my Lord Chesterfield's axiom that refined people will no more advance civility to a bear than money to a bankrupt.

At this moment a footman announced a Mr. Falkland, and the Duchess, whispering to Sir Robert that 'twas a young spark but just arrived from the grand tour, he turned to survey him, lest in the new-comer he should find another Medlicote.

Oh for a dozen Ranulphs in this hour of need! for a score of such faithful recruits to assist the labouring ship!

But this Mr. Falkland was not of the same kidney. The affectations and effeminacy were all there, but not the sterling qualities beneath. 'Twas writ in his vacant visage and retreating brow and chin, as, unabashed by the general rising of so large a company, he minced forward.

'Your servant, Duchess,' he said. 'I've been dining at Lackit's with a polite campany, and naw I'm as rumpled as if I'd slept in my clothes. Ah, my Lord Belvedere! your most humble. I had the pleasure of being acquainted with your lardship when I passed through the Hague.'

'These travelled boobies, with their sham dialect, are insufferable!' murmured Sir Robert. 'As unlicked whelps they're better. Was not his papa, think you, Duchess, a musk-cat, his mother an essence-bottle?'

'Pray be seated!' cried her Grace sharply, as if to say, 'Young man, since you pretend to be well-bred, don't keep the company standing.' 'Let me introduce you to Mrs. Belfield, whom you will hand to supper presently.'

The young lady made a deep curtsey, the youth as low a reverence, while Ranulph, who had expected this honour, favoured the interloper with a stare.

Pamela, in her element now, went off at a tangent; for here was a third string to her bow, who languished already in orthodox fashion, and pressed the tips of her fingers.

'What?' she said. 'Oh yes! I dote, don't you, upon assemblies? My heart bounds at a ball, while at the opera I expire! Cards enchant me, and the music of dice puts me out of my little wits! And don't you like hazard? Dear hazard!'

'I do indeed!' drawled the young man. 'Dath it not impart a flow of spirits? I perceive that your ladyship and I shall become the greatest friends.'

'And the play? Do you not adore the play?' tittered Mrs. Belfield.

'Aye! and the players too!'

'What? Oh, these dreadful men! Have you already made the acquaintance of the hussies?'

'Gadso! Nothing easier of approach to a man of fashion.'

'A lie!' muttered Lord Byron, who gazed on this caricature of himself with the disconcerted air of a cat that looks in a mirror. 'Some that I know are not to be reached with a long pole, and a still longer settlement!'

'I know 'em all,' pursued Mr. Falkland. 'Introduced myself with a pinch of bergamot. Next day sent a boxful and some verses. To the hour dropped in at rehearsal to be thanked, and desired that my name might be used for all the chocolate-house affords. This opened all their hearts so wide that in a whiff it cost me fifty gannies in fans, gloves, maffs, and orange-water.'

'I wonder what men can find in the baggages!' sneered the Honourable Pamela. 'There's that Whig player who made such a scene to-night, dear Lord Chesterfield!—was not her effrontery prodigious, Lord Bolingbroke?'

'Stap my breath!' interrupted Lord Belvedere, covertly glaring at his imprudent offspring. 'To such beauty all is permissible. May I be sunburnt if she isn't handsome!'

'And as good as beautiful,' bluntly remarked Sir Robert, who, callous as regarded himself, objected to hearing Mrs. Philpot's name so lightly bandied.

'Not of such insolent vartue!' drawled the young fop, with a meaning smile.

'Oh, fie! I protest I must be scarlet!' tittered Pamela behind her fan.

Sir Robert frowned, and muttered:

'He hath been a year in Italy, to bring back nothing but a fool!'

The Duchess, looking grave, moved to the door, and, having given an order, returned to the glittering group that had gathered round the speakers.

Lord Byron bit his nails in wrath, and grumbled half aloud:

'I doubt she was willing enough that night but for the untimely rescue. But to sell smiles to such a beggarly younger-brotherish runagate! Drown me if I believe it!'

'You are wrong,' returned Lord Forfar, who overheard. 'He hath money, doubtless; and the players will do anything for money.'

Spindleshanks felt that Gervas must be right, and cursed himself for the fiftieth time in the matter of that thousand pounds.

'Such jests,' said her Grace severely, 'should be kept for your velvet sparks at Garraway's. Supper is served. My Lord Bolingbroke, I reserve you for myself. If you please, we will lead the way.'

The diversion was well timed. Pamela was in a mischievous mood, irritated by her parent's signals. Just as if she did not know how to behave as well as he! If she chose to call the Dawley farmer by endearing names, sure she knew what she was about! 'Twas so seldom he was seen at a gathering, that it behoved her to be vastly winning.

Lord Byron evidently was hard pressed to control his temper in the presence of the ladies; while young Mr. Falkland was calmly wrapped in the contemplation of his own image in the pier-glasses.

The aspect of a sumptuously furnished table turned general attention to a blither channel than disputes about an actress. The ladies took their seats—the gentlemen, of course, serving them standing, and, when glasses and plates were full, slipping into the places by their sides.

Her Grace, with my Lord Bolingbroke on one side and Sir Robert on the other, seemed vastly tickled by the contiguity of the political rivals; and the natural foes, entering into the whimsical situation, made believe to forget the *Craftsman* and the fight, which on the morrow would commence with redoubled vigour.

My Lady Suffolk, somewhat bewildered, had the tact to engross the master of Dawley, or Sir Bluestring's usually imperturbable *bonhomie* might have pricked his bag of venom.

Mrs. Belfield kept a seat next to her for the dear Jacobite, thereby disgusting her papa. Mr. Gay flapped about like the busiest of butterflies, waiting on all.

'Separate those two,' the Minister suggested in an undertone. 'That jade is in a wicked vein—I see it in her eye—and will lure that foreign cub to mishap.'

The Duchess, glancing down the table, saw that he was right, and summoned the delinquent Falkland to approach nearer. Jealous Medlicote slipped into his seat, and thus Mrs. Belfield found herself between her two aspirants.

Foiled in a laudable attempt to sow dissension, that young lady, turning a cold back on Ranulph, devoted herself to the cultivation of the Jacobite. 'Twas a fine occasion for pumping him—one that must not be lost. So, assuming a subdued and serious manner that befitted the subject, she delivered herself of a warm panegyric on Lord Forfar's friend, which surprised the guileless conspirator.

'What a *gentleman* is my Lord Bolingbroke!' she murmured. 'Good breeding carries a dignity with it that commands golden opinions; while the reverse invites familiarity. Even fallen and disgraced, no man ever said a pert thing to him; while to his coarse neighbour there, in the snuff-stained coat, who ever said anything civil, except in flattery?'

'This from you,' exclaimed Gervas, round-eyed, 'who belong to the Court party!'

'Alack!' sighed Pamela meekly, 'we poor women of quality have been taught nothing to earn bread withal but the tambour and the harpsichord, and may not starve. We're as base as the players with their purchased smiles—pretending sympathy when our hearts are far away!'

Gervas was grieved; for indeed 'tis a hard fate for a sensitive high-born woman to eat the bread of servitude if rendered so intolerable as she hinted.

'Oh, how I detest it all! And the usurping upstarts!' she sighed; then whispered softly: 'He over the water doth hold no female Court.'

'When he comes to his own he will,' replied Gervas, with equal mystery.

'Nay; that will never be!' returned the artful one. 'The cry has ever been "To arms! To arms!—now or never!" and then they fall to bickering over their little dignities, and the precious moment passes.'

'Too true!' sighed Gervas. ''Tis the curse of poverty that warps men's souls and bends them crooked.'

'Who knows it better than I?' murmured Mrs. Belfield. 'But you should feel pity for a woman's weakness, which must be denied to man. Oh! if I were a man!' she said, kindling, then sighed again and lowered her eyes; while from a distance my Lord Belvedere glared in vain, grinding in impotent rage his newest set of teeth.

The heart of Gervas warmed to the poor girl, and a thought crossed his mind for which he chid himself till he reflected that in unequal wars all weapons are permissible.

'I feel you are to be trusted,' he said, as she gazed languishingly at him. 'We bide our time, but are not so sluggish as you think. The besotted folly of that man there plays into our hands. Hitherto his craft hath baulked our every step; for men can be weak as well as women, and gold is god of all. If you speak your mind—and I know you do—you might be of signal service to us.'

Lord Forfar's voice trembled, and, the words sticking in his throat, he lapsed into silence. His better nature revolted against making the suggestion which was in his mind to a woman whom he really liked.

But Pamela's quick brain guessed the half-spoken hint. Had it not occurred to her own mind some time since that a nest might possibly be feathered by disclosing to the other side that which passed within St. James's? There she knew that all was tottering. If she only could be sure that t'other side was less unstable!

Afraid in her inmost heart of the single-minded Jacobite, she had felt that 'twould never do herself to propose a bargain from which his lofty eccentricity might revolt. But now she perceived that even he could stoop, and felt relieved to find him human.

Without another word she reached out a little hand under the table and touched his with a pressure that meant volumes. Had Lord Belvedere known of it he would doubtless, forgetting to be lackadaisical, have hurled something at her head and caused a diversion.

Yet, after all, as matters stood, she could lose naught by such a bargain. Was it not at her will to choose how much to divulge, how much to hide, while groping a way in the dark labyrinth? Moreover, would she not gain gratitude from him by the throes of a seeming sacrifice? Might she not rivet his chains by a thousand alluring airs of confusion; of wishing to speak and yet not daring; of sacrificing prudery, modesty, what not, for the good of the sacred cause which she knew he cherished so religiously?

Why, with feminine skill might she not seem in his eyes a very Joan of Arc? At present everything was to be gained, and nothing risked by a secret compact. Why not, if the side of Hanover finally won the day, turn round and make a merit of divulging what Gervas might drop? How like a self-sufficient coxcomb of a man it was who was old enough to have learned wisdom, to glare across the table emptily, while she, his much more clever child, was spinning such a web in her trim little head as his common male brain was incapable of conceiving!

While the Honourable Pamela and my Lord Forfar were apparently billing and cooing like a pair of enamoured turtle-doves, her other neighbour, Mr. Medlicote, found it mighty dull. He sullenly ate his supper, then drummed with his fingers on the cloth, reflecting that he had gathered nothing wherewith to amuse the Queen.

He was glancing towards the door, considering how, unperceived, to make escape before the party moved to cards, when it suddenly opened, and two ladies entered quietly, whose aspect made him start. He had seen them oft before.

Without moving, the Duchess smiled and pointed with her fan to a place that chanced to be empty beside Lord Belvedere. The younger, with winning grace, swam into the seat; but the other, shrinking from the brightly lighted table, apparently much disturbed, moved into the shade, and sat there watching.

Pamela happened to look up.

'Really,' she remarked, 'her Grace is too eccentric! 'Tis to please Sir Robert, I suppose, that she admits the Whig mountebank in such familiar fashion to sit among the quality!'

It was indeed Mrs. Philpot whose unceremonious entry at so late an hour caused a hubbub of surprise. We know that, in pursuance of a mysterious message from her patroness, Barbara, instead of seeking early rest to cultivate fresh roses, had looked out her smartest frock, and, accompanied by her mother, had made for Burlington Gardens.

My Lord Belvedere was in the seventh heaven. Not a jot did he care now for Pamela's sly tricks! Had not the reigning beauty twice repulsed him, thereby inflicting serious wounds upon his vanity— even refused to nod in public? And here she was now by his side, looking distractingly lovely, as with the *bel air* she took off her long gloves of chicken skin, and allowed him to pile up her plate.

This was indeed entrancing. Had he not displayed his false teeth for her behoof in vain across St. James's Street from White's bow-window? He would deserve slight and oblivion if he failed to improve so opportune and valuable an occasion.

Seeing her at close quarters for the first time, his practised eye examined her lineaments. How admirable was this clearly chiselled profile! how refined the small transparent nostril and firm chin, the graceful curves of the long neck; how rich the glow of the full bosom, so lavishly displayed and cunningly set off by a low square bodice of white silk.

Her head was made up Dutch, with cockades of ribbon on the sides and diamonds across the front, powdered thinly to show grey. All down her back were escaloped lace ruffles, mounted each with a jewelled solitaire; while as for her hoop, 'twas of that becoming wideness which forbids a vivacious damsel to turn round in an ordinary sized apartment without oversetting everything like a whirlwind.

'Elle est bien; même très bien!' muttered my lord. 'Jolie comme un cœur—faut la décrotter.'

'Milord est trop aimable,' demurely responded Barbara.

'A Parisian accent—fiends and spectres!' cried the diplomatist. 'I forgot that angels were not banned at Babel.'

'Nor brought up in a French seminary,' replied

the actress with a laugh that showed such a row of pearls as outdazzled my lord's best set.

'Do you know,' he said, 'that you are quite different from all the tragedy-queens whom I have ever known? Excuse *franchise* due to unstinted admiration, and therefore flattering. However skilful their efforts at concealment, they can never disguise the odour of the lamps. An aggressive tinge of the *parvenue* always lies in the folds of their brocades. Some, I know, are of good birth. Your actor Wilks, I am told, is of superior lineage. The civil wars contributed many sons and daughters of good but impoverished houses to the English stage when royalty came home. Sure yours must have been too loyal to the Crown?'

A shade of sadness passed over Bab's cheek, and she was silent.

'She doesn't so much as know who was her father,' he thought. Then, perceiving that he stood on treacherous ground, like a man of the world he changed his tone, and plied his neighbour with shafts of lightest raillery, in which he was joined across the table by Mr. Medlicote.

Bab speedily recovered her equanimity, for who more fit to cope with an army of triflers? Soon the laughter in her vicinity rippled loud and free in jocund waves, inviting general attention.

Was this likely to be pleasing to the Honourable Pamela? Hardly. Was it not pestilent in a low theatre wench to appear in highest society with the *aplomb* of a genuine patrician? She dared to shine—and to outshine Pamela! This required putting down, and at once: for, having been grievously spoilt, llke all low hussies, she was becoming insufferable.

In the public walks one expects to be elbowed by all sorts of trulls; but at Queensberry House! Really King Charles had set an odious precedent in the matter of Nell Gwynne, and the Duchess would ere long regret her imprudence. And here was my Lord Belvedere—her own father, whose years, at least, were respectable—making an exhibition of himself, and disgracing her by whispering things into the creature's ear, which doubtless were unfit to be heard; aye, and filling her glass and his own with objectionable frequency. Mrs. Belfield girded up her loins to put down the creature.

Indeed, the new-comer wore her fine-lady airs as if to the manner born, and showed no signs of shyness.

In obedience to her Grace's whispered behest Sir Robert had merely extended, as she passed, a podgy hand. My Lord Bolingbroke, rising with formal dignity, had honoured her with a ceremonious obeisance, while my Lord Chesterfield drew a delicate line by the manner of his salutation between the artist and woman of quality. A reviving buzz of recognition and pleasure swept over the party, which, conscious of heat and surfeit, had grown dull. This apparently mortified young Mr. Falkland, whose darling desire to seem as much at home in town as an old rake was frustrated. Who could this new arrival be who was on familiar terms with all? Lord Byron, grinning from ear to ear, was waving jewelled fingers. My Lord Belvedere had seemingly summoned from their repose the three Graces to array his old carcase for conquest, as in a shrill treble he kept repeating:

'Slip through my lungs! A little glass! I protest you shall! or stap me, I swoon with disappointment!'

It behoved the would-be rake to rally his scattered forces, for the lady was absolutely acquainted with everyone in the room except himself.

'Your Grace's relative?' he drawled. 'I judge so by her beauty. The likeness is striking. She doth well to be defended by a dragon.'

'Your servant!' shrieked her Grace, whose eyes danced with fun. 'Gay, out with thy tablets and indite an ode upon the likeness 'twixt me and my fair cousin. My cousin, said you? or was it niece?'

'Sister, it should be,' smirked the infatuated fop. 'Two cherries on one stalk never were more alike.'

'Lord! What a world we live in!' cried the Duchess, suddenly serious, as, like a soldier grounding arms, she rapped down her fan upon the table.

'Thus is't that half our modish crew spend their life in inventing lies that t'other half believes! Mr. Falkland, you are young enough to learn a lesson without hanging your head. This sister of mine, as you suppose, is the Whig player, whose favours you have been vouchsafed without knowing her even by sight!'

With that the impulsive Duchess rushed to the astonished actress, and clasping her in both arms, kissed her on either cheek.

'My dear,' she said, hoarse with unwonted emotion, 'pardon my little stratagem! This lad, to raise his reputation at the expense of yours, traduced your character. I knew he could not have seen you at the theatre, for he hath been in England but two days, and you have not acted for a week. He will no doubt crave humble pardon, and be more careful in the future. An amnesty! Come—to cards! You, by your own confession, Mrs. Belfield, adore the knaves—on pasteboard.'

In dire confusion at the discovery of his meanness, Mr. Falkland awkwardly bade farewell, and slunk away with tingling ears; while my Lord Forfar, indignant and disgusted, sang after him a requiem.

'How paltry a form of vanity,' he said, 'it is to try and raise one's self by lowering a woman! If the insidious charge be true, 'tis ungenerous; if false, infamous!'

Relieved somehow that the charge against Mrs.

Philpot should have been signally refuted, he looked down into Pamela's face for approbation, and she could scarce keep her fingers from slapping him.

'Oh, these virtuous enthusiasts!' she thought; 'how they deceive themselves by windy platitudes! There's little of nobility, no doubt, in thieving a woman's fame; but is there more in coaxing them to wrong? This preacher would make a tool of me, a spy—would sacrifice his grandeur for the cause, if need were—and if I am skilful I shall win the prize for which I angle; and yet he doth not see how base the temptation is that he is throwing in my way! Well, 'tis a comfort that those who blow themselves out with principle, and those who profess none, are much on the same platform after all!' And with this consoling conclusion Mrs. Belfield gathered her skirts about her, preparatory to adjournment to the card-room.

The hussy had scored a point, which was regrettable; but 'twas not necessary for a lady of rank to assist at the player's triumph.

The surprises of the evening, however, were not over. Before conducting his lady from her place, Lord Forfar, as the gallant way was, proposed a toast, and gave 'The accomplished and bewitching Pamela Belfield.' 'Twas drank as usual, standing; and then my Lord Byron gave another, 'The peerless Barbara Philpot.'

Now Pamela's besetting sin, or one of the many

that strove for mastery, was pride. Her old father's open flirtation with a player under her very eyes was distasteful to Mrs. Belfield. She coloured, and with disdainful gesture cried in a loud voice:

'Poh! His lordship's breeding leaves somewhat to be desired! Cannot he do better for a lady of fashion than name after her a paid Jezebel!'

There was a murmur of consternation, but the angry damsel heeded it not.

'Her own scullion can insult her any day,' she sneered, 'from the gallery on payment of a shilling!'

Bab started and turned livid. Taken aback by the cruel charge which an unknown man had brought against her, she had gratefully accepted in silence the kindness of the Duchess, feeling thankful and softened, less lonely than usual. But now again to be insulted, and by this audacious skirmisher!

'A Jezebel,' she said, facing Mrs. Belfield with full as haughty a mien, 'may well be harnessed with a demirep!'

The Duchess was much put out. The conduct of her guests was suited to the tavern rather than to a polite hurricane. A vulgar brawl like that of grooms in a boozing-ken! Worse—for the belligerents were women. Pamela, convulsed with passion, seized a brimming glass, and would have flung it full in the blanched face of the beautiful fury opposite, had not Lord Forfar wrested the missile from her grasp.

The men stood irresolute, not knowing what to do. 'Twas a mercy the table stood between, or there would have been a sad rending of headclothes. My Lord Belvedere, whose expensive peruke was awry and his eyes a trifle over-bright with wine and excitement, endeavoured to bridge the chasm.

'Never mind the baggage,' he whispered, clasping Bab's waist and endeavouring to draw her down. 'I'll punish her at home: Sit—you shall! Udswoons, sweeting! those ireful lips must be melted into smiles again!'

The old gentleman, suiting action to words, proceeded to deliver a salute, crowing the while like a venerable rooster.

Punish her at home, would he? Pamela, trembling and gasping, turned to Lord Forfar. 'Prithee take me hence,' she said, choking with resentment, 'till my lord hath finished with his trollop! Will some one lend me a chair? I wist not that in your Grace's halls I should rub shoulders with posture-makers!'

With a solemn curtsey the Honourable Pamela swept over the threshold, across which the Duchess inwardly swore she should never step again. Trollop and posture-maker and Jezebel, forsooth! Which of the twain was the aggressor? Insolent minikin, to dare to teach her, the Duchess of Queensberry, whom she should invite as guests! Verily, the plebeian-born had shown more dignity than she who boasted of her quality! And her old father, too, was pretty nearly as bad, for, half intoxicated, he had pulled the actress on his knee ere she could elude his grasp.

'If I'm overbold, sweeting,' he hiccupped, 'your charms must bear the blame. Love and assurance, you know, are as inseparable as a lady and her vizard.'

It added no little to the Duchess's chagrin to mark the grins of amusement which puckered the visages of both Bolingbroke and Walpole. The latter cried 'Bravo!' when his little Whig so promptly returned tierce for carte; and now his sides shook with merriment, for the affected old fop cut a ludicrous figure in his character of Lothario, and the Minister awaited, with malicious eagerness, the swingeing box on the ear which must reward his too delicate attentions.

Rapidly as the scene progressed, no one had noted the growing concern of the dame who occupied the shade. Wringing her hands, with scared eyes as though she beheld an apparition, Madam Walcot rose and rushed into the light.

'For dear Heaven's love, desist!' she cried. 'I had a fear of this! God knows how I've prayed and wept! Lord Belvedere—George!' she moaned. 'Do you not know me? Sorrow and sore repentance have seamed the cheek you once thought fair!'

Lord Belvedere scrutinized the features which, kneeling on the ground, she raised imploringly to his, and murmured with astonishment:

'Hepsibah!'

'Yes—Hepsibah!' echoed the wretched woman. Then, turning a hasty glance of terror upon the expectant company, she gathered, as it were, her courage in her hands, and with a supreme effort wailed:

'Do not touch the child! Miserable sinner that I am! She is your daughter!'

Had the massive chandelier fallen into their centre, amazement in varied phases could not have been more clearly depicted upon every visage. In horror and dread of she dared scarcely figure what, the confession of her own shame had been wrung by iron Nemesis from the blue lips of the devotee.

Lord Belvedere, slowly unclasping the writhing Barbara, seemed for a moment stunned; while she, turning from red to white, became stricken by wonder into stone.

The Duchess was the first to recover composure, as, tapping her fan upon Sir Robert's sleeve, she jubilantly cried:

'I knew she must be a sprig of quality!'

The Minister, with lamentable lack of morals, was equally charmed. On one side at least his favourite was of gentle blood.

'Nature,' he answered, with exultation, 'hath

formed her for high circles; Fortune must accomplish the intent.'

The old fop slowly awoke, and, sobered somewhat, realized what the scene meant for him. The respectable Mrs. Walcot, crushed by the words that had been wrenched from her, lay cowering upon the floor. With a pang he felt that he must look ridiculous, and pushed Bab from him with one finger. All eyes were staring at him, all faces seemed marked by gibing puckers. Ere a week was out hundreds of doggerel sheets would flood the town, of which he'd be the hero—the printshops would teem with jests.

His stony heart was pierced. How he longed to chastise that sobbing Magdalen who, by a public scene, held him up to obloquy! For an old woman to state that she was once your flame is not flattering to your own years. Still the jeering array of eyes stared full on him, wondering what he would do. It behoved him to back out of so absurd a predicament with all possible grace and speed. Oh, how he would have liked to drub that silly old woman—that Hepsibah of his youth, who ought to have known better than to be so scared at bugaboo! What if he were unwittingly embracing his own daughter? Odds heartlikins! She might have known that 'twas for merest fashion's sake, to stand well before the town with the popular idol. Why not have writ a warning note, instead of shivering and moaning, eating out her stupid old heart in foolish apprehension, then blurting out her more than idiotic folly before his friends?

But Hepsibah always was the veriest ninny! To think that after—never mind how many decades—the crows should fly home to their nest! My lord sat pondering so long that the circle, on tiptoe, began to murmur their conjectures. How difficult to escape from such a dilemma without loss of dignity! Lord Belvedere whistled a stave, opened his box with deliberation, and after taking a pinch, brushed the dust from his steinkerk, and dropped into his beauish manner.

'Split my windpipe!' he drawled. ''Tis more plaguey vexing to me than to your Grace to have upset your earthquake. We must make the best of it, or yon gentlemen will quiz me. A nobleman, whatever he feels, should keep his countenance serene, since emotion begets wrinkles. Your ladyship never had cause for fear, for I never cared a fig for *you;* nor, since you belong to me, am likely to begin. But it befits not the daughter of Lord Belvedere to be a player, however charming. If your Grace's footman will be so obleeging as to call our coach, I will conduct my daughter home.'

My lord, tucking his hat under his arm, offered the extreme tips of his white attenuated fingers with orthodoxly filbert nails to Mrs. Barbara, and led her slowly forth as if about to step a minuet.

So soon as the door closed on them, her Grace

observed heartily that no one could have emerged from a quandary with more consummate breeding after so sad a commencement. 'Twas a vastly refreshing end.

So the green baize had fallen on the actress, who was raised out of reach of Crump. How would the Honourable Pamela feel when presented to her sister?

CHAPTER II.

A RISE IN THE WORLD.

THE Duchess of Queensberry would not have been a child of Eve had she not tossed all night, gnawed by curiosity to know the result of the 'scena.' Half a dozen times she rang up her first maid for a dose of cordial, till that much-enduring person felt half inclined to administer laudanum instead. 'Twas wonderful! How true had been her instincts! One who leans upon a single virtue should always be mistrusted; and Madam Walcot's exaggerated assumption of shocked propriety was, as might have been expected, only a cloak for a *faux pas*. When young, Lord Belvedere must have been a rake in red-hot earnest, and, oblivious of the effect of decades, must have goaded her fears even to the wrenching off, with her own hand, of the mask of second nature.

The poor gentlewoman must have suffered anguish

ere she could have brought herself to this. Well, 'twas her own fault if the company stood open-mouthed. Had she not buckramed herself so tight in pinchbeck modesty no one would have been astonished; for when modish belles set so little store by reputation, 'twas the most natural thing in the world for a plebeian—if a plebeian she were—to fall a prey to a lord. The secret of Barbara's distinguished manners was out now. Democrats may prate rubbish, but blood will show itself. In dogs and horses 'tis admitted; why not then in men and women? Part of Mrs. Philpot's success had been due to the *je ne sais quoi* that stamps the patrician. ' 'Tis a volatile essence—intangible, yet there.' When Bab had declaimed in tragedy everyone had vowed 'twas mighty fine, for the imperious slut, with the exquisitely cut profile and lofty stature, was satisfying to the eye in a thousand piquant attitudes of scorn and triumph. 'Twas a stilted convention which was accepted as edifying and statuesque, though altogether out of nature. But when she appeared in comedy 'twas otherwise. Her Lady Betty Modish, Lady Townly, Lady Brute, were the genuine article. 'Twas the polished mirror held up to nature, the real fine lady, just stepped out of the most fashionable drawing-room.

What Lord Belvedere had said, with perhaps undue candour, was true. However gifted the ordinarily circumstanced actress of whatever period, the cloven foot will out. The Duchess plumed herself on her discernment. With all his affectation and his frivolous nonsense, my Lord Belvedere had shown in a difficult moment that he was worthy of his coronet; and Bab was his true daughter. At first sight 'twas strange that of the twain the one who was legitimate had been found wanting; for verily Pamela, betrayed by evil passion, had behaved like a fish-fag! Perchance the mysterious Madam Walcot was of gentle blood. As to Pamela's mamma, 'twas known that my lord, when Minister at Lisbon years ago, had made a *mésalliance* with some adventuress or other, who happily had died in giving birth to Pamela.

The Duchess sniffed when reflecting about Mrs. Belfield, for 'twas too bad to have made a vulgar scene at a polite hurricane! Before she belonged to the Queen's household, had she not lived mostly with the Duchess? The villa at Bushey being too dull for a single girl, had not her Grace obligingly advised that it should be closed till the end of my lord's diplomatic mission, while his daughter abode with her?

That Lisbon wife must have been very low. Pamela had shown at least half of the cloven foot, and the Duchess burned to know what had happened as to the other half when the sisters met. So she popped on her morning mask and scarf, and was carried in the plain chair, which she generally used for auctions, to the select street off St. James's, with the little green wicket into the Park, where the town *ménage* of the Belvederes was established.

What a triumph for Bab, after having been treated to 'trollop' and 'Jezebel,' to step into the family parlour and claim a place in it! Did Mrs. Belfield scratch her eyes out? Did she go into hysterics, and swear by the household gods that two such discordant elements could not exist under a single roof?

Had my Lord Belvedere whipped her as she deserved? That there was nothing but wind inside his pericardium everyone was aware who knew him. For him *les convenances*—a delicate and highly burnished worldly punctilio—took the place of heart and conscience both; and it must be allowed that he who surrenders himself to such cool and calculated guidance makes few errors. *Les convenances* had told him at once that his long lost and neglected child having been handed to him thus dramatically, 'twould never do to reject the unlooked-for present.

'Lord Belvedere's daughter must not be a player!' Her noisy surroundings at the 'Lock of Hair' had amused him often as surveyed from White's chocolate-house; and punctilio had said to him when he discovered who she was, that Lord Belvedere's daughter's chamber must not be a rendezvous for beaux *en déshabille,* who were waiting to be, or had just been, shaved. His first impulse was a correct one. Boasting of no principles, would he continue to act rightly, or would the shrill ravings of Mrs. Belfield affect his subsequent conduct?

There must have been an awful uproar, either in the middle of the night or this morning, and her Grace, peering up at the house, was half disappointed to find that the windows were still whole, and that the roof still held its place. Her Grace's discernment had deserted her. In putting two and two together, she was wrong. Lord Belvedere's foppishness was but a crust, thickened, no doubt, by habit. His diplomatic career had shown that when needful he could be as cunning as the fox. 'Twas little probable that any amount of vapours or shrieks on the part of the Honourable Pamela would turn a settled resolve.

The footman who opened the door was no less dignified than usual, as he ushered her Grace into the morning-room. There was not a single chair or looking-glass broken. The two sisters sat like lambs on either side the hearth as calmly as if they had thus sat during all their lives. Bab was frowning at the last number of the *Craftsman*. Pamela, whose nose was a little red, pricked her needle into her tambour with an occasional sniff, and a concentrated viciousness which told unutterable things.

'My dears,' cried her blithe Grace, 'behold the Garden of Eden! Where doth the naughty serpent conceal himself?'

Mrs. Belfield had succeeded in schooling her exterior to a decent extent, but was too sore as yet for banter.

'If you mean my father, madam,' she replied, sending the tambour spinning on its wheels across the floor, 'he is above, with a *posse* of tailors and steinkirk-makers. I'll say you are here, and, if not too much engrossed in selecting a wig for the Park, he will doubtless attend your Grace.'

With that Mrs. Belfield stalked majestically from the room, and slammed the door behind her with such violence that all the chaney danced.

'Bravo, Bab!' the Duchess laughed, with a hearty kiss. 'No poisoned dagger? No henbane in your chocolate? I congratulate your ladyship.'

'This is kind,' Bab answered gratefully. 'I feel so strange — almost happy; yet awe-stricken and shocked.'

'You will regret the incense of the stage?' suggested the Duchess.

'Oh no! I never loved it, save as a means to an end. How grieved poor Wilks would be to hear me say so! When, mindful of Oldfield, he talked as he did to her of the exacting goddess, I always felt guilty, and a charlatan.'

'While the heart slumbers,' gently said her Grace, 'so doth the soul.'

'The goddess who claims your heart's blood!' mused Bab. 'I was often told, before I wist he was my father, that he never had a heart. Why, then, should I have? And if no heart, how can it give its blood?'

'Better so,' declared the Duchess. 'The road to the Walhalla's strewn with bones and bitterness. Sorrow sleeps lightly—beware of stirring her!'

'I have always so longed for a father,' Bab went on, relieved at thus unburthening herself.

'Desirable, no doubt,' acquiesced the Duchess, 'if they love their offspring. Look at the romantic whale, for instance, that carries its young under its arm! I vow I've always thought that the love-affairs of whales must be vastly touching!'

'Perhaps because 'twas a blessing denied to me I had the longing. Do you know I am bent upon his loving me?'

'That wig-block?'

'Even so.

'More than he ever will the other. And you pretend to have no heart?'

'I can't tell,' smiled Bab. 'Just think! A love-child confided to chance, thrown out without experience to sink or swim! To be able to love some one, and be loved again, would be so delicious, if only for the novelty. Is it not curious that I am doomed to possess one parent only?'

'As how, you fantastic paradox?'

Then Barbara fitted the puzzle together so far as she had mastered it. Hepsibah, so my lord had narrated in the coach as they drove home, herself a motherless waif, had been smitten with him, and he with her, when both were young. Growing weary of a prize too easily attained, he had accepted a mission to Portugal; and, having married there, was no little disconcerted by the pursuit of deluded Ariadne. His wife was a Spanish gipsy, and jealous. To avert a possible tragedy, he compromised with Hepsibah for a sum of money; and was relieved to hear that, on the homeward voyage, she had captured one Walcot, the captain of the vessel, who had been *épris* on the way out.

To facilitate matters, my lord had taken the child, whose existence told an inconvenient tale, and had sent it to France to be forgotten. My lady dying shortly afterwards, his mind reverted to this babe; and he instructed his steward to arrange for the accumulation of a certain modest sum, which was eventually to serve as dowry. But Hepsibah, married and settled, was to interfere no more.

After a lapse of years, the steward wrote to his master, who was still abroad, to say that Hepsibah had broken the compact; that, professing indigence, she had sought out her daughter, and discovered herself. My lord, incensed, had thereupon replied that the girl was to choose; and if she clove to her mother, the dowry-money was to be paid down, on the clear understanding that neither would ever trouble him again.

Fearing that the choice might go against her, Madam Walcot had so craftily managed that Barbara never learned so much as who her father was. 'Twas only on leaving school she had learned her name was Philpot. With the money the Richmond toy-shop had been bought; and on my lord's return his ex-mistress had been in agonies lest, through her public and prominent position, which the mother had never contemplated, father and daughter should meet, and an explanation ensue, to the detriment of the devotee.

When the imbroglio was further complicated by his lordship's enrolling himself under the Diva's banner, she was so horror-stricken that, goaded by despair, she had herself blurted out the words which 'twas her interest never should be spoken; and had thus brought down on her own head the avalanche she had so clumsily attempted to evade.

It was evident now why she had striven to the best of her weak powers to keep her daughter from the stage. Had she remained in the toy-shop, 'twould have been easy to get her away on some pretext should his lordship appear at the Wells; or, if necessary, she might have moved with bag and scrip. But Barbara, independent and self-willed, had taken the bit between her teeth, and was beyond control long ere my lord's return.

Finding, by a few leading questions, that the disobedience of his child had been through no fault of hers (for the careless steward never troubled to go himself to France, or to explain her father's prohibition), Lord Belvedere decided to take his daughter back again; but on the understanding that never by word or note was she again to communicate with mamma. The deceitful old lady was to keep the toy-shop and the money, and go about her business; while Bab was to go home with papa, and make herself agreeable. It is possible that but for the public explanation, his decision might have been different.

There were other motives, too. Pamela, he had discovered soon after arrival in England, was not to his mind. She was shrewish and not pretty, and woefully disrespectful. As a philosopher, he might say to himself that young jades are good for naught but to put men out of humour ; yet 'twas displeasing to find his admonitions treated with undisguised contumely, and raisings of sharp shoulders. Had Bab been ugly and shrewish, he might have behaved at the hurricane less like a perfect gentleman. It was flattering to his *amour propre* to find that the deserted bone of his bone had made for herself a position; that she had wormed her way unaided into the best society; had become the darling of the public; and, in all ways, did credit to her parentage. He might disapprove of the position she had carved as derogatory to the blood of Belvedere; but 'twas vastly engaging to be able to pluck the idol from its pedestal, and saying, 'This is my property,' to put it in his pocket.

This being the exact position of affairs, he was by no means loth to place so fair an ornament by his fireside; and felt also a malicious pleasure in punishing, by the same stroke, the too snappish Pamela.

Now, Pamela was sharp of wits as well as of tongue and shoulders; and, after the first cold shower of displeased surprise, saw clearly that she could not fight, or remove the thorn from her flesh. Thanks to his long absence, she had no real hold over papa any more than Bab had. If he had taken a hussy to dwell with them, she could have rushed to the Queen and screamed. But there was nothing to be done upon the tumbling from the sky of an unwelcome sister, save to mask her spite and wait; which, like a wise damsel, she forthwith proceeded to do, reserving the tears of abortive rage for the privacy of her virgin closet.

Thus did it come about that her Grace, instead of stepping from her chair into pandemonium, had walked into the Garden of Eden; and in her delight she swore with oaths, like the woman of quality that she was, that the pocket-poet should mend his pen, and put it all into a play.

We can all endure dreadful things for a second, which, spread over a lengthened period, become intolerable. The attitude of the Belfield family promised well as a beginning, but the three personages concerned became speedily aware how difficult it is to keep heroic resolution hot when off the boil.

Ere many weeks had passed Eden showed signs of transformation into a howling wilderness, and my lord discovered that his bachelor home abroad was less uncomfortable than his English family *ménage*. By means of the hundred microscopic ingenuities of feminine artifice, Mrs. Belfield succeeded in filling the chocolate of sister and parent with henbane, and in flourishing the poisoned dagger to her heart's content; and though Bab had by general consent been christened angel and adorable seraph, she was not given to meek endurance. Aristocrats can stab so genteelly, and with so little mess of gore! Mrs. Philpot had had her own way so long, had been so flattered and worshipped, had grown so accustomed to see every idle whim gratified before it was half expressed, that 'twas a terrible effort to sit serenely still under Mrs. Belfield's arrows.

'Twas nice to be an idle *belle à la mode*, and to feel that in a sideway fashion she really belonged to the quality. But after all the satisfaction was insipid. Barbara had changed her bed, and had lain in it a short while only when she became conscious that—like the other which had not proved satisfactory—it had its crumpled rose-leaves.

Little by little it dawned on her that the new

position was as hollow as that of Diva had been, and that there were grave drawbacks attached to it. To fence with Pamela might be refreshing. As to winning the affection of Lord Belvedere, she might as well have made love to Westminster Abbey as attempt to obtain that which did not and could not exist. In the genteel household sympathy of nature to nature was conspicuous by its absence.

There are things (not many) which a woman of quality must not do. Lord Belvedere's acknowledged daughter must not accept bank-bills, and bracelets, and earrings from the beaux. In this much they must be kept at arms' length; and what is the use of being a real lady of fashion without ample means? As a Diva it had never been necessary to know the value of guineas and bank-bills. Had they not showered in without the asking? Bab liked cards and dice as well as any, and attending auctions and so forth. A lady of fashion may cheat at ombre and hazard to the extent of forgetting to pay; but she may not plunge a hand into the bank and boldly pocket the stakes. Now in this Pamela had the advantage, for she had never possessed money to spend, except in driblets, and, much as she hated poverty, had from childhood been accustomed to the concealing of it, and the schemings of ways and means. Not so Bab, and the gripings of a lean pocket were like irons harrowing the soul.

Of course she was too proud, even by the winking of an eyelash, to allow her sister to perceive the source of disillusion, or permit her to guess that so soon as the gilt had worn off a little, she regretted her Bohemian liberty. The happier she was in her new home, the more would Pamela be vexed; and so, with dissatisfaction gnawing her heart, she carolled up and down the stairs, executing merry roulades and humming artless ditties. As all the world expected them to scratch like cats, 'twas tacitly agreed to balk the malignant by angelic displays of affection, always on the overflow. They were to pose as sisters should, with arms gracefully twined. They were to kiss and call one another by a thousand endearing epithets; dress in the same colours; go about together as though a sudden affection had sprouted up like unto Jonah's gourd. And yet the two ladies loathed one another with the most sturdy healthy hate, for which there were endless causes.

'Twas a little awkward, at first, the getting over that episode wherein ' trollop ' and ' Jezebel ' had been so freely bandied; and yet in the polite world do not folks cultivate the shortest of sight and memory? Pamela's love before acquaintances was as lavish as could be desired; but her hatred, of the two, was the stronger, and certainly most enduring.

My pen blushes and jibs, almost refusing to write that the Honourable Pamela Belfield was made to play second fiddle. She was edged and pushed into the position of *younger* sister! The superb beauty overshadowed—snuffed out—the haughty bedchamber-woman on her own territory now—on her own hearthstone! Oh, crime unpardonable, never to be forgotten, to be avenged with butchery and massacre and torment and thumbscrews and pincers on the earliest available opportunity!

Not only on her hearthstone, but even in the palace. Yes—actually! To please Sir Robert, who was full of the romantic bit of gossip, the Queen deigned to summon Mrs. Philpot, invite her into the Holy of Holies; absolutely instructed that unduly honoured minx to attend twice a week in her most killing costume to impart her own grace and refinement to mesdemoiselles the young princesses.

Was everyone to bow down before this brazen idol? Mary and Louisa were to be taught the use of their arms and the management of that feminine weapon, the fan. 'Twas terrible to have to hear that hated voice in the royal ante-chamber, as Mrs. Commander-in-chief shouted to her willing recruits, 'Unfurl! Ground fans! Recover! Flutter fans!' and so on. And Mary and Louisa enjoyed the lesson so much that the coming of Mrs. Philpot was watched for eagerly.

The Queen averred that the bubbling of merriment was as good as a ray of sunshine. Oh, the audacious, familiar, overbearing, *vulgar* trollop! aye, and Jezebel too! How gladly would her dear sister have flung her out of windows after the manner of that queen, for the dogs to scrunch her bones!

I protest that I shudder as, at this awesome moment, I peep into the inside of the outraged Belfield. Being possessed of bowels for you who read, I will refrain from divulging what I see within that Golgotha. When Bab exhorted their Royal Highnesses not to mumble, or when tickled by a jest to allow people to see down their august throats, or to stoop, or make a noise when feeding, Mr. Medlicote, who dubbed himself Aide-de-camp to the bewitching General, closed his lips and threw back his shoulders and stood in dancing-master Des Noyer's most unexceptionable attitude.

He applauded her lightest sally, roared with laughter over her meanest quirk. Oh, poor Pamela's inside! Ranulph Medlicote—just think! One of her own tame fishes, and she had but two who were likely to be landed; one of the men whom she elected to twit and snub and otherwise harry and maltreat, as it behoveth skittish maids to behave to possible future husbands.

Did Jezebel propose to pitch a flaunting tent in Naboth's vineyard; did she intend to appropriate titbits and favourite morsels? It almost seemed so, for, in her new *rôle* of *quasi-grande-dame*, Barbara dared, assuming a lofty tone, to lecture Gervas himself—the standaway Lord Forfar, who was so fond of believing the worst.

She presumed, sometimes almost seriously, sometimes in an off-hand manner, to take him to task anent the sacred Cause, gibing at his most cherished tenets, holding under his nose for admiring imitation that lump of corruption, Bluestring. 'Twas amusing to give ear to her light, careless prate, and Lord Forfar was amused—not shocked and indignant as Pamela would have had him be.

Lord Belvedere's daughter, made much of by a usurper's wife and received by rank and fashion, was one person; Mrs. Philpot the actress, exposed to temptations, the butt of rakehells, was another, even to the single-minded Jacobite—always excepting when she went too far, which, alas! she sometimes did.

Not that Pamela need have been jealous, for Gervas looked on Mrs. Barbara much as we consider the tiger-lily. We stand for a moment and admire its stately proportions and vivid colouring, and then pass on without a thought of culling the flower and wearing it as a posy. The charms of Mrs. Belfield, you will say, were not of a retiring and modest order. No. But between the two women there was, in the Scotchman's eyes, a vast difference. Independent Bab proffered unasked advice, and took him in hand, dragging him sometimes a step or two against his will; for hers was the stronger nature. Pamela the artful craved guidance, offered herself as a willing tool for the bringing about of a desired end; posed, as it were, like Iphigenia arrayed for sacrifice. After that unsigned compact at the Duchess's, the tender finger-squeezings under the table, she made much of Gervas, sending him nebulous messages, making dark assignations for the purpose of divulging something which invariably turned out to be naught. In her character of traitor in the Hanoverian camp, she had little to divulge which was not known all over the town; but in such a case sure the will may be taken for the deed—the sweet interest of a sympathizing bosom for information of a specific value.

In spite of all precautions, Pamela had shown herself more than once to my Lord Forfar in her sherbet condition—acid and seething; and he had been compelled to admit to himself that the tartness on these occasions was a trifle too pronounced. But then, was it not ingenuous thus to wear the heart upon the sleeve? What man, I must ask you, would not be flattered by perceiving the influence for good of his presence over an esteemed object? For when his dark eyes turned with reproach on the skittish maiden, she coloured and simmered down. Bab, on the contrary, always behaved worse than before. How many men have been caught in a cleverly laid net while they thought themselves improving and instructing?

Much as she resented her father's admonitions, Mrs. Belfield was not so silly as to neglect warnings. She knew her tongue was sharp, and kept it under control in the presence of Gervas as much as was possible—that is, when not goaded to madness by the covert taunts of Barbara. When he entered the room, her features softened into amiability; the steely sparkle of her eye became more mellow, and she was by no means averse to let him guess the cause. Under these circumstances, it was clearly the duty of a well-meaning, if not too clear-sighted, man to exert for the patient's behoof the occult power he seemed to possess. When, a little hand gently laid on his, she twittered in a corner of the Cause, he almost felt that she was a brand plucked from the burning by him—that he had converted her from evil ways; and, rendered thus unsuspicious, would hearken with eagerness to petty tittle-tattle of the backstairs, from which, had he not been blinded by party, and dust deftly thrown, his uprightness would have recoiled with horror. Too guileless conspirator! His spy and disciple wound him round her finger; and, in process of time, she might probably have led him, while he deemed himself the leader, to any point she wished. Not that she desired at this minute to do more than keep him in tow, waiting on events. Was it not exasperating, then, that interloping Jezebel should show signs of annexation; should summon the booty of her own sword and spear to desert his allegiance, and tie himself to gilded Juggernaut to be crushed with the press of victims?

When imperial Barbara irrupted into the corner where the two were cooing, and swam away with Gervas, Pamela was so numbed with helpless fury that she sat choked and passive, without the feeblest repartee. What could she do to oust this kill-joy? Dagger and bowl, indeed! No torments invented even by Spanish monks and bishops in the cause of holy religion were sufficiently complete and excruciating.

Bab, on her side, was urged by a variety of motives. In the first place by a sly spirit of mischief. She knew that 'twould annoy Pamela to have her communings disturbed; and, considering how well the latter succeeded in annoying her, 'twas a matter of legitimate reprisal. She was not quite aware of the fact, deceiving herself somewhat with the idea of a good action when, in sooth, it was in this a mean one. And yet she was actuated a little, doubtless, by a desire to wean an honest man from under the influence of such a woman as she knew Pamela to be.

From the first he had held a high place in her esteem, and 'twas piteous to see him innocently led astray by the arts of her despicable sister. If they were conspiring in corners—and they certainly must be conspiring—it was clear that Mrs. Belfield would be the gainer; for Mrs. Belfield was not one to sacrifice a hair of her head for any Cause, however pure and worthy. And Bab was quite certain that the patriot was duped—that his Cause was far from noble—that 'twas lighted, in his eyes, by a delusive glamour which shone upon it from himself.

It had come upon Bab by degrees that, however well it might be to escape from the sham and tinsel of a stage-life, she must occupy her mind and time with something; fill up by her own efforts the emptiness which still oppressed her. How was she better to achieve this, considering the bent of her friendships, than by plunging into the sea of politics?

Having reigned as a theatric Diva, why not, under changed auspices, exert her beauty and talents for the behoof of the great Whig party? What a worthy triumph it would be to detach so respectable a personage—one on whom the Dawleyites relied—from allegiance to what she sincerely believed to be a rotten Party, and convert him to Whiggism! She knew how base was Bolingbroke—how odious the persons were who could stoop to invent such lies as daily poured from the *Craftsman*. She could trace with such clearness the good points of Walpole, that 'twas a constant marvel to see how one so English in his blunt bull-dog sturdiness could be so misinterpreted and misread as Sir Robert was now. No doubt she beheld the Minister through spectacles of her own colouring; but every woman sees every man through spectacles of some sort, either grey or rosy.

Perchance the reverence which she could not help feeling for Lord Forfar was due to her own imagination. On his side, the Jacobite showed little sign of being influenced, for his spectacles were dun-coloured. Impulsive and domineering, there was something within her—the Bohemian element, possibly—which always clashed with his square-toed ways of thought and bearing. She could not help it, and it made her angry with herself when, provoked, she was impelled to sallies.

The impulse to cut short a droning platitude by upsetting a tea-table with a pretty show of *gaucherie*, or by placing a foot upon a chair with a display of too much stocking, was too strong for control; and when the freak was followed, as it invariably was, by a pained withdrawal on his part into the shell of propriety, she could have taken his handsome head and banged it against the wall.

If there was something antagonistic between them 'twas beyond her power of removal. He might never grow to like her, but he could not prevent her from respecting him, and admiring him too. Did it not behove her, then, as an honest and energetic woman, to protect him by any means from Pamela, and coax him, if it might be, into the proper fold? Of course it did. Thus was it that she persisted in interrupting *têtes-à-têtes*, until the younger lady almost resolved to snap up Lord Forfar out of hand, prospects or no prospects, through sheer acerbity and spite, if only to baffle Jezebel.

The Duchess of Queensberry, to whom the doings of the household were fully as entertaining as a comedy, resolved to speak to Bab; for to her, as an unbiassed spectator, it appeared naughty to employ weapons bestowed by Nature for the public good on so mean an object as the appropriation of Pamela's man. All the world could see that Lord Forfar was dangling after one or t'other of the young ladies, and since he seemed to prefer billing in corners with Mrs. Belfield, 'twas not proper in the other one, whose train of beaux would reach, if she thought well, as far as Paul's, to interfere in the quiet wooing.

Bab, when taken to task, was amazed.

'What!' she exclaimed, 'not tease the men? Would you rob beauty of its prerogative? Fiddle-de-dee! Fancy such as I pretending to a union with Lord Forfar!'

Though she made believe thus lightly to waive the point, it set her thinking; and her thoughts wandered away into their least pleasant channel. How dreadful it would be if Gervas was really wooing Pamela! And yet, why should it be dreadful? Might she never learn the lesson thoroughly which she had sternly resolved to teach herself? Quasi woman of quality she was; but as regarded future prospects her position was by no means ameliorated.

More than ever now must she abandon ideas of marriage; for the bend sinister would stand in her way every bit as much as the being a player had done. How often must she repeat to her stubborn heart that she was only aping the *grande dame*? Just as before she resolved to marry nobody, so must it still be. What did it matter? For the veriest mess of pottage she had marred her future; and yet not so; for she was quite sure now that she disliked the stage, and all connected with it. Her position at present was vastly blank and inane. Well, there was no way out of it. When beauty waned she would take a leaf out of her mother's book. Meanwhile, 'twas only fitting to enjoy life as much as circumstances would permit.

Argue thus as she would, this suggestion of the quiet wooing was mightily distasteful to Barbara, and she assured herself with vehemence that 'twas all talk about conspiracies, not Eros. Why, without at all desiring to have him herself, 'twas clearly a duty to prevent so direful a catastrophe. So sterling a man deserved a better helpmeet than that vain creature! Of course 'twould look ill for Bab to interfere; but would not the Duchess warn him? If only he could witness the daily wranglings and quarrels, sure he would flee, fingers in ears! Yet no!

'Twas better to leave things to work themselves out. That Gervas could have serious intentions with regard to Mrs. Belfield, her sister Philpot declined altogether to believe. And having thus made up her mind, she dismissed the unpleasing subject.

Perhaps if we were all turned inside out, shown in private moments as seen by our valets, but few of us would ever reach the altar. 'Twould be curious, as a matter of statistics, to ascertain how many couples have regretted their fate during the second week of the honeymoon.

When my Lord Belvedere married the gipsy, Pamela's mamma, he very speedily discovered that he had caught a tartar; and was no little relieved when she flitted to the next stage on the journey. And very likely the lady was as glad to be quit of him, for in private the diplomatist was not a genial companion. He was given to dyspepsia of a morning, and his temper was not improved by the reflection that his successes were less brilliant than of yore. 'Tis not delightful, even to the most amiable, to get up and look in the glass, and behold there wrinkles and grey hairs and creases about the chin and neck.

When his lordship descended to breakfast in a white damask cap and splendid gown of brocade, he was invariably cross. Pamela was always peevish, too, at that most trying hour; profoundly indifferent to feelings.

She was unlucky at cards as well as in other

things, and the subject of dross, save when he won it, was woundily unpleasant to her parent. One morning when Bab came down, fresh as a daisy, shortly after her conversation with the Duchess, she almost wished that Gervas could be present to observe his fellow-conspirator.

'Guineas!' my lord was querulously complaining. 'Stap my vitals, but I like your insolence! You've been long enough now in the market to have found a purchaser, but must make an idiot of yourself upon the losing side. Such drivelling imbecility! You know that ready money's scarce. Tenants are such rogues and fop-makers are such thieves; and periwigs are so ghastly dear that 'tis as much as I can do to find us all in gloves and hair-powder. Go on the highway and take a purse, as Charlotte Charke did; you're bold enough!'

'If father and child are not to talk of money,' perked miss, 'I can't see what they've to do together!'

'Death and furies!' roared my lord. 'Daughters, methinks, are built up of pride and paint and buckram and disobedience! If I could find a woman who was not impertinent, I'd marry and hope for a son to vex you!'

But Lord Forfar was not aware of these amenities. Dropping in a few hours later at the same moment as Mr. Medlicote, he found my lord about to saunter forth into the Park, in all the glory of rejuvenescent smirks and a new fop-cover, while the sisters were smiling sweetly.

'Oh, bad men, bad men!' shrieked Mrs. Barbara, flourishing a gazette to display the roundness of her arm. 'Just to think of what some of you are capable! Sister Pam takes in the *Craftsman*, and I needs must peep because I ought not, although it grows so vile that Ketch should have his will with it. Just hearken!'

And in tragedy tones the ex-Diva read aloud:

'" Is this accursed Minister one of those bubbles of fortune who, because he hath hitherto escaped, thinks that he will always escape? Verily, not content with wounding a free constitution of government, he resolves that it shall expire under his administration. If he succeeds in his sacrilegious designs, he may hope for impunity perhaps for his grey hairs, and be suffered to languish through the infirmities of age, but with inward remorse more pungent than even any suffering that he hath inflicted on so many multitudes. By entailing servitude on the race he will inflict indelible infamy on his memory." Really, my Lord Forfar, you should blush for him who fathers all this flummery.'

''Tis harmless,' asserted Medlicote composedly; 'for it overreaches itself and defeats its intended purpose. Decent people grow disgusted. We should be thankful to my Lord Bolingbroke for showing his true colours.'

'Indeed, I am ashamed,' Gervas admitted, with some confusion. 'My friend o'ershoots the mark, and yet his soul is earnest. 'Tis but excess of zeal.'

'Remember what Richelieu said of zeal!' laughed Ranulph. 'A few more such poisonous vomitings and we'll carry Excise in spite of you.'

Gervas was looking hopeful to-day, and the heart of Barbara warmed to him.

'Of course we shall carry Excise,' she replied gaily. 'And my Lord Forfar will be dragged by the dirty hands of gaolers through the streets in chains, as Christopher Layer was twelve years since. Come now, be wise while there is time, and take heart of grace to shout with me, " Down with the Pretender! Long live King George!"'

'If beauty leads our foes, then are we undone indeed!' laughed Gervas. (Pamela was charmed to perceive how bright he was, and plucked up her own spirits accordingly, with a furtive glance at Bab.) 'When I'm dragged to Newgate like an Algerine captive, will your ladyship be sufficiently interested in my fate to deign to look upon the show?'

'I gape on traitors like an orange-wench?' cried Mrs. Philpot. 'You forget that, like sister Pam, I'm a fine lady; too busy with routs, drums, earthquakes, hurlyburlies, and cards to gaze on any spectacle of blood excepting a bear-baiting.'

'Are your lives thus filled?' Gervas inquired with

a lengthening countenance, the sight of which made Barbara redden.

'Our lives,' she laughed, 'are like the lives of others—are they not, Pamela? We play basset or hazard each night at four assemblies; then sup till three, and dance till five, and chatter till six over the follies of to-morrow. Leave names at twenty doors; take a turn in the Mall to cross verbal swords with the sparks; send for a pretty fellow out of a chocolate-house, coquet for half an hour in a mask, and make the zany treat us without so much as seeing our faces; then to the auction to make the gallants buy fifty costly nothings for which we've no occasion. That is a fine lady's day—is it not, sister?'

Mrs. Belfield bit her lip, for Bab was trying to discredit her before the punctilious Jacobite.

'Speak for yourself, my dear,' she sneered. 'We know that your inclination is as wide as a coffee-house door, for all the beaux who choose to frisk in and out of it at will.'

This was a lamentable display of acidity, and Mrs. Belfield's ire rose in that she had slipped into the trap.

Lord Forfar's brightness had departed, and he remarked with sad sententiousness:

'Your friends, the three Miss Mostyns, spend such a day, no doubt. A bad example.'

'Not my friends—Barbara's,' Pamela hastened to state.

'Who frequent the politest houses,' interrupted Bab.

'Having no reputations to lose, it matters not what they do,' snapped Mrs. Belfield.

'Wicked!' screamed Barbara, in extremest glee, since my Lord Forfar elected to be glum. 'Of course we are wicked; but you men are worse, for having more courage than we, your sins are more impudent. The men of the mode! Do they not ruffle, hector, fight, drink, blaspheme? While we, poor cowards, can do nothing more brave than lie, backbite, and cheat!'

'Two more charming sinners——' Mr. Medlicote began.

'Nay,' cried incorrigible Bab; 'no comparisons, please, betwixt two sisters. Remember the bad painter who, having limned a cock, drove all the real poultry from the neighbourhood!'

It was always thus. She monopolized all comers, and started inopportune subjects. What had Mrs. Belfield done that this overpowering jade should have been foisted on her? 'Twas a consolation that Gervas was looking upon Mrs. Philpot with ill-concealed disdain. His unusual cheerfulness on entering meant something; or did it not? 'Twas certain that now he had relapsed into the most dismal dumps. A female Machiavel never lets slip a chance of feeling the ground.

'Tell me, Mr. Medlicote,' Pam tittered airily,

'when my lord here and his adherents are drawn Towerwards, what form will your triumph take?'

'None at present,' replied Ranulph, with composure, 'save joy at Sir Robert's victory, as becomes a faithful henchman.'

'A henchman! and you used to pretend to be ambitious! Oh, how I despise a man,' sneered pettish Pamela, 'who throughout his life is content to carry candles and set chairs!'

'Meaning me?' laughed Ranulph. 'I have time to wait, and am never in a hurry. For the present my ambition is centred in devotion to a friend, his gratitude sufficient guerdon. A cloud rests on him, but it will pass, believe me. If not—well, although I never could hope to soar to the level of my Lord Forfar's self-sacrifice, I should not be surprised, should Sir Robert fall, were I to stick to him.'

Pamela stared at the Vice-Chamberlain, scarce daring to believe her ears.

'He hath staunch supporters,' observed Gervas, brightening again. 'But in spite of all we've a good chance. 'Twill be a hard tussle. In town the mob heaves for riot; in the country the squires have the toast pat, "Property and Liberty, and no Excise."'

'Without comprehending the Shibboleth,' drily suggested Ranulph.

'Never mind,' retorted Forfar, gleaming forth like the sun between April showers. 'Believe me or not, the job's in as fair a way as a boy to be a rogue who's bound to an attorney.'

Absolutely a joke from the Scotchman! Something most unusual must be on the carpet to account for so weird a prodigy.

Pamela felt that she must know more, or explode then and there upon the spot. Rising with well-assumed languor, she slowly moved to the open window, and stepping out on the small square of garden, beyond which was the Park, was rapt in contemplation of the landscape.

'My Lord Forfar,' she screamed presently, 'your taste is ineffable, and you've not commended my new beaupots.'

So direct an invitation from a lady was not to be refused.

'There can be no doubt of our success,' whispered Gervas, as he sniffed the flowers, 'if our supporters are as staunch as his.'

The female Machiavel was right, then, in guessing there was somewhat in the wind.

'' Tis ill groping in the dark and talking riddles,' she retorted.

'I will speak out, for I can trust you, and you may prove of greatest service,' hurriedly whispered Gervas, as she adorned his coat with a blossom. 'He will be betrayed in spite of his supporters. At a signal from me, the soldiers on whom he relies will turn on him. He is to be kidnapped.'

'Walpole!' whispered Pamela, scared.

''Twill be done during the riots which our agents will foment. At a given hour 'tis essential to know his whereabouts. There's where your help may prove consummate. A summons as from the Queen—anything your genius may devise. Once taken, there will be a panic in the palace, and the royal family will fly; for what can they do without him?'

'As James II. did,' mused Pamela; 'and James III. will be proclaimed.'

In reversed order, history was to repeat itself. Here was news indeed, fully sufficient to account for jubilation, even in the glummest.

Already Mrs. Belfield beheld herself a duchess, and saw in glittering perspective a career akin to that of the great Sarah. How, then, would she fling back upon his head her father's gibes; avenge an hundredfold the stings of Jezebel! A dynasty o'erturned, and she the instrument! Something within fluttered, and stirred, and swelled—a latent monstrosity that took the place of heart.

'I am wholly yours—to the last gasp devoted!' she said, in a tremulous undertone. 'Yours only! Command.'

'Ready money's sadly lacking,' mused Gervas aloud. 'Most grievous, for his bonds are as yet hardly marketable. A thousand pounds at this critical moment, to pay the kidnappers, would be worth a million.'

'Alack! I've none!' replied rueful Pamela. 'A woman of quality hath so many calls.'

'Who'd lend a thousand pounds would earn a thousand thanks,' groaned Gervas. 'In sooth, I've dire need of the poor sum—a paltry thousand pounds!'

Bab, whilst flirting with Ranulph, wondered what the two could have to say over the beaupots, with heads so close together; and, urged by mischief, she skipped thitherward like unto the frolicsome foal, accompanied by Mr. Medlicote.

'A thousand pounds!' she echoed to herself, catching the last words. Trying to borrow of Pamela! Sure 'twould be as wise to beg of the shoeblack at the corner! How wrong was the Duchess, inveterate match-maker! Money and not love! 'A thousand pounds!' she repeated unconsciously aloud.

Gervas started, finding himself overheard, and strove in a blundering way to avert suspicion.

'We men are out at elbows sometimes,' he laughed, 'as well as the carding ladies. King Hoyle is seldom kind.'

This was a deliberate falsehood, and from the lips of Gervas, the upright, who never touched a card. Across Bab's mind there flashed a sudden vision of the squalid Clink where, searching for Charlotte, she had come upon the man in the blue surtout. 'An angel, not a lord,' had said the turnkey. Noble fellow! Still the secret benefactor of the hopeless, rescuer of the despairing!

He had twitted her on that occasion with the charge of idle curiosity. How fine a revenge was placed in her hands now! She, as well as he, could keep a secret, and revel in the secrecy. He persisted in believing the very worst of her, then, did he?—indulged in impertinent rebukes anent the friends she chose to select!

If she chose to know the demirep Miss Mostyns, 'twas her business. Yes. She would be splendidly revenged by an anonymous donation of the very sum he required. The thanks of the poor prisoners would rise to the footstool, and she, though my lord in his self-sufficiency knew nothing of it, would claim a share in the incense. He wanted money for his noble work, and craved it of Pamela. A serpent for a fish; a stone for a loaf. That was all he could get from her to whom he elected to be partial.

With an exulting glow to which her breast was strange, Bab bethought her of the packet of bankbills so mysteriously left in her apartment. True to her resolve—the more firmly kept for Honest Jack's suggestion—she had retained the bundle intact, hoping to find an owner. Now that her life was changed that hope was gone.

What better employment for it than to assist this man in his holy work without his knowing it?

What an inward satisfaction would be hers, when the prim look of displeasure lowered over the Scotchman's visage, to murmur :

'He thinks me a lump of self. Yet 'tis I whom he should thank; I, the hard and harsh, the unutterably worldly and corrupt!'

Mrs. Philpot was so delighted with the whimsical fancy that she seized her unwilling sister by the waist and whirled around the room.

'Fairies tripping in a magic circle,' suggested Ranulph.

'Not so!' shrieked Bab. 'Next week is Southwark Fair, and we want practice. I vow I'd die of spleen if baulked of Southwark Fair. Will ye join us, my Lord Forfar? Byron shall go, and the Mostyns. I'll gather such a troop as was never seen on Bankside, and there, as Queen of Revels, will hold high carnival.'

Still with superior strength she whisked round panting Pamela; then, out of breath, flung her aside and struck a burlesque attitude.

'Yon mildewed knight!' she cried, so loud that promenaders in the Park turned round, 'shall wear a Whig cockade, and drink King George's health. 'Tis a bargain that we go to the fair together. Shall it be so, my lord? The bigot, you know, always makes the boldest Atheist!'

CHAPTER III.

'EXCISE.'

THE high spirits of Gervas, and the exultation of Mrs. Belfield, if a trifle premature, were not unjustified, for Ranulph's words were prophetic. As the spider unrolls a web from its own bowels, so did sedition grow by feeding on itself; and the wiser portion of the community looked grave, for disorder is easy enough to raise, but when tumult is in full swing no one may guess the end.

Fond of his bantling as he was, Sir Robert reluctantly saw that public opinion was too strong for him in the matter of Excise. Sure of his own singleness of purpose, he refused as long as possible to believe that the swarm of anonymous scribblers would succeed in stinging easy-going old John Bull to frenzy, forgetting that when once the vulgar have digested a suspicion, 'tis as hard to work on them with common-sense as to hew blocks with a razor.

He knew that the free importation of the necessaries of life would, by rendering them cheaper, reduce the price of labour. He knew that by reducing the price of labour, the price of home manufactures would be decreased, and consequently—from the fact that we could afford to undersell other countries—that the demand for our goods in foreign markets would be increased. No one could be more aware than he of the short-sighted injustice of opposition to his Bill, but he was the last statesman to struggle for the national good at the expense of himself and his. As things were, the fate of the House of Hanover had come to be bound up with himself. The Dawley junta knew that there was no hope for them but in a general overturn. Their reigning Majesties had resolved loyally to stand by their Minister, and it behoved him, for their sakes as well as his own, to stamp the young life out of the monster which threatened to devour them all.

But 'twas a bitter pill Sir Robert was called upon to swallow! How was he, having gone so far, to back out gracefully without loss of prestige? Agitation was becoming fiercer every hour. The scene at Drury Lane had showed the direction of a steady adverse wind, and the friends of Government perceived that but for the Diva's presence of mind, the Queen herself might have been publicly insulted, the match set to the powder-barrel which would have blown them all into space.

Although the Bill had been finessed through the first stage, it could never become law. Obedient to Bolingbroke's paid host, who concealed their insignificance under incognito, and yet made their way by dint of numbers, the country became mad-drunk. Pamphleteers, 'like so many screaming grasshoppers held by the wings, shrilled every ear with noise.' On all sides the wildest opposition was raised by those to whom agitation is a business; and there was no standing against the flood of petitions which poured in from all large towns. The unpatriotic Minister whose degraded brain could invent such a horror as 'Excise' was branded by the foulest epithets, the bitterest invective; and my Lord Scarboro', speaking to the King of what passed without, bluntly said, ' I'll answer for my regiment against the Pretender, sir, but not against the opponents of " Excise!"'

Hence it was plain that the hot cinder must be dropped with as little finger-burning as might be. Walpole's bull-dog spirit for an instant was disheartened.

'The floor's too slippery. I cannot stand on it,' he said mournfully to the Queen, who replied:

'Decide what is right and wise. We know that all the bustle springs from private enmity. Settle, and we obey. If wrong or premature we ought honestly to own it; for 'tis only to admit that we are wiser at night than in the morning.'

The calm devotion of the Queen was touching, for the poor soul was sadly worried. The King's fitful explosions of humour fell as usual in the first instance upon her, and 'twas hard to have two crosses to carry—one placed upon her back by a husband, the other by a son. For Frederick, Prince of Wales, who for a while had been quiescent, seized the moment of tribulation at St. James's to trot forth and become actively obnoxious. He laboured under the delusion that his own popularity had outlived that of his parents; that if they were overset he might usurp their shoes—an absurd idea which was fostered by Bolingbroke whilst laughing in his sleeve, for no engine might be despised whereby stones might be flung at the arch foe.

The coal could not be dropped, but must be laid down gently, Walpole prudently decided. The many-headed becomes insolent and unmanageable when it discovers that it is feared. To put the tail between the legs and run away would only set the pursuing curs howling louder than ever, since the thing Britons despise above all else is cowardice. The City of London was to present a petition, among a host of others, praying to be heard against the Bill; so extraordinary and unusual a demand—contrary, indeed, to all rules and orders of the House—that it could not be dropped at once, lest the merchants, aldermen, vintners, what not, might be possessed by the unfortunate notion that they only had to arrive in a stream of coaches to coerce Parliament to their bidding. Others besides the City worthies supposed as much, for during the progress of negotiations the purlieus of Westminster were a constant scene of turbulence, the lobbies and adjacent open spaces in almost undisputed possession of King Mob. Early in the struggle the οἱ πολλοί had come down to threaten members; and finding unstemmed riot with its perquisites more amusing and profitable than commonplace labour, formed themselves into camps and dwelt therein like squatters.

Although loyal to the Minister and calm to the outer world, their Majesties suffered anguish within closed doors. Little George snapped alternately at wife and mistress both by day and night, till both wished themselves well buried. Like many better people he deceived himself, imagining that he was very stout and absolute because the two patient Griseldas pretended to admire and never contradicted him; whereas he was as much led by the nose as the meekest spouse, and was, with all his personal bravery, as arrant a political coward as ever wore a crown, and as much afraid of losing it. Much as he loved Hanover, and little as the English or their country delighted him, a surreptitious packing of trunks and departure in the dead of night was not a pleasing prospect, and what

Gervas and the Dawley junta had hoped for appeared likely to come to pass.

Walpole's policy, as we have seen, had always been of the Cæsar or nothing kind. No sooner did a friend show signs of soaring, than he was instantly ejected from office. Pulteney seemed like to be revenged, for the rats were running away from the labouring vessel ere it should settle down under the billows. Many who had received benefits chose this moment to desert their chief. Mutiny and disaffection showed their heads, and, as Ranulph told the Queen at her toilet, Bolingbroke's party at St. James's was more numerous and active than at Dawley.

Who so charmed at the way things were going as Mrs. Pamela? How wise, how prudent she had been! The star of Gervas was in the ascendant, and she was binding him to her side with hoops of steel. On the question of the City petition — whether it should or should not be considered in Parliament — Gervas had spoken, and spoken well, and the Government majority was so small as to be equivalent to defeat.

Prudent as she deemed herself, she could not conceal her exultation, posed as a Queen of the lists delivering the wreath of victory; whereat Bab's laughter was so loudly ribald that, stung into incaution, the woman of the bedchamber made sundry admissions which quickly reduced Barbara to gravity. That Mrs. Pamela should flirt with the interesting Jacobite and gabble in corners about the Guy Fawkes effigy was one thing, but that she should seriously conspire with him for the destruction of the Whigs was quite another, and she all the while in the Queen's service, fed by the royal hand!

Mrs. Philpot held a low opinion of Mrs. Belfield's character; but that she should turn out to be so mean as this was painful, for after all she was the child of the same father. Lord Forfar's attitude was fraught with dignity, and Bab liked him all the better for it: he was independent and consistent, bent on succouring the weak; but that he should elect to pour his confessions and views and confidences into the lap of such a double-faced thing as Mrs. Belfield was deplorable.

Mrs. Philpot was assailed by sharp twinges of anger in that one so worthy should be so little a man of the world; should be so lamentably deficient in judgment. What should she do under the circumstances—in her lately assumed *rôle* of champion little Whig? Denounce her sister to the Queen, to Walpole? Not till less desperate measures had been tried. She would argue with Pamela; if need were, implore Lord Belvedere to intervene—to insist that at least she should resign her post and unfurl her banner openly. To a generous mind a snake in the grass is the most despicable of objects. Alack! Neither lady displayed genius for conspiracy. That

Pamela could not keep her triumph to herself was sad in so sharp a female.

That Bab should suppose for a moment that words of hers could have any effect save the opposite of that intended, 'tis woeful to her chronicler to confess. Bab spoke her mind with the airs of an elder sister, and Pam retorted with bile. There was a terrible rumpus between the ladies, which almost led to that breaking of furniture that her Grace had so eagerly anticipated; and when my lord was summoned to intervene, he turned the vials of his wrath in equal measure upon both.

'What have women to do with politics?' he inquired testily. 'Why cannot they confine themselves to tea-table tittle-tattle, beaux and furbelows?'

That Bab should have found favour in the eyes of Majesty was good; that the First Minister should display such unwavering partiality was excellent from a social point of view; but that she should occupy her pretty head with Excise was preposterous and grotesque.

'Twas all over the chocolate-houses that she had stood in her chair with the top raised t'other day at the entrance to St. Stephen's, offering a kiss to members as they passed if they would promise to vote with Sir Robert. Duchesses, of course, may do anything; for their rank is as good a cover as charity.

Lord Belvedere declined to believe that a daughter

of his, who in some things had shown herself to be clever, could have been capable of such an act—her position being anomalous and demanding tact and caution—but there was no smoke without fire, as all the world knew, and she must have been guilty of something foolish. But whatever that might have been, it could not equal the inconceivable folly of Pamela. Stap his vitals! her papa would like to apply his clouded cane to her thin shoulders. Could she not find a better *prétendu* than that friendless and penniless Scotch pauper? Even if t'other side came in, was not the ingratitude of the House of Stuart notorious?

The Pretender would rouse himself, possibly, from a chronic state of drink to mumble thanks; but he would not be lavish of coin, and without coin of what use are honours? Sure he and his had painful experience of that—odswind and thunder! At all events, she had no business to coquet with Apollyon so openly until 'twas clear that the angels were in flight.

To Pamela her papa's tirade was inflammatory instead of soothing. To be lectured in this blunt style before scornful Jezebel, the domineering elder sister! It was true about those kisses—so like a trollop! Though, as the embraces of actresses are to be bought for sixpence, 'twas like the impudence of a hardened hussy to offer her cheap favours as a bribe! As to the Scottish pauper, he was not so friendless as my lord supposed. Only t'other day he was praying for a thousand pounds to emulate Bluestring's tactics for the benefit of the Cause, and lo! the desired sum in bankbills had dropped like manna from the sky. Who would dare say after that that the Cause was not a holy one?

To listen to Pamela prating about holiness would at any other moment have stirred the latent humour in Bab's nature; but her heart tightened, and a throbbing spasm choked her utterance.

Could this be true—so unwisely divulged? Under the impression that Lord Forfar required the sum he named for his benevolent labours in Southwark, she had sent him the mysterious packet by a secret hand. And all the while 'twas sinews of war that he required to undermine her champion!

Why had she not guessed it—she who was so fond of advising? An ignominious feeling of folly surged up, which was bitter to endure. In the first moment of distress she almost resolved to take papa's advice, and leave politics to wiser heads. But then, if she had unwittingly done Sir Robert such a wrong, was it not her duty to fight for him all the harder?

When next she visited the palace she sought the advice of Medlicote, told him of Gervas and Pamela, and in return for the stab thus inflicted upon the *amour propre* of that young gentleman, received herself another wound, which set her reeling.

'Twas Sir Robert himself who had deposited the

bills under the china centrepiece, and now they had been used against him ! By the light of Ranulph's hint she saw it all. The bills formed part of the annual bribe to his Grace of Bolton; but Walpole, knowing his *protégée's* extravagance, and pained by the brutal speech of his secretary about the debtor's prison, had impulsively bestowed them upon Bab! And with such unusual delicacy; while she had supposed it was only another item in the long list of Byron's insults!

Mrs. Philpot groaned in spirit. Well, what was done could not be undone, for now her means were straitened. But she must strain every nerve and muscle to assist her benefactor in this his moment of extremity.

In the palace all were dejected enough. The Princesses Mary and Louisa, depressed by the general gloom, went through their fan exercise with apathy. Bubbling merriment ceased to echo in the ante-chambers. The never-ceasing clatter of the King's wooden heels upon the parquet as he paced and fidgeted wrung the Queen's nerves, till, able to bear no more, she took to her bed and buried her head in the pillows. And yet ignorance of what passed without was torture.

From time to time knots of rioters ran down the street, and bearding the sentries as they turned the corner, yelled, ' Liberty, and no Excise !' At night the glare of flames glittered through the glass upon the walls of the royal chamber, as the mob danced with obscene chorus round two burning effigies—a fat man and a fat woman—Sir Robert and her gracious Majesty.

How would this end? Opposition, feeling its strength, was disinclined to be generous. When was St. John generous? By a dozen deft manœuvres he fanned the seething populace, urging them to terrorize the Court by their excesses, while Gervas and Pulteney and Chesterfield thundered in Parliament, rending the obnoxious measure. Copies of the *Craftsman* were found under the Queen's plate, in her scrutoire, even within the harpsichord whereon she tinkled, striving after oblivion of the present. Who was the cruel wretch who could be so pitiless? Bab knew who it was, but held her peace. So long as Pamela's darts were no better feathered she would not betray her sister. Appetite comes with eating. Undiscovered, unpunished, she would grow more bold. What would the next move be? How soon would it be necessary to unmask her? It behoved Bab to watch and wait.

Pamela, though her home was within a stone's throw, slept now at the palace, for the Queen's anxiety grew more oppressive hour by hour, and the mob had begun to amuse itself by wrecking well-appointed chairs. Her Majesty would have her Vice-Chamberlain rung for at all hours of the night, and keep him talking on one side of the door, which opened just upon her bed, while she conversed on the other, asking a thousand questions as to what he thought, feared, hoped; as to what Sir Robert had said last; and Pamela, listening, faithfully reported the budget.

Walpole seemed to have lost faith in himself—ominous sign!—for he sat, so Ranulph told the Queen, for an hour at a time motionless, hat pulled over eyes—he who used to be so genial and so buoyant!

'We must sound the retreat,' he had instructed his henchman to explain, 'and retire in good order by means of a postponement; then amuse the public mind with a royal marriage. The mob love a show. The fanfares, and trumpet-blowings, and pageantry will divert the fickle public from the unfortunate Bill; we will have the troops out and coerce the populace, and all will be charming well again.'

So these were his tactics? It must be the business of the Dawley junta to prevent the orderly retreat by an attack upon the commanding officer. The mob must be further inflamed by being informed about the soldiery. The weapon of the people was to be turned against themselves? A pretty thing! Were Britons to be enslaved? Who had been right about the standing army? So long as Walpole reigned, Liberty was indeed in peril. His classic lore suggested to the bedizened pedant the act of Constantine at Verona as worthy of imitation. The great Emperor—refinement of severity—took from the vanquished soldiers' hands their swords, and had them converted into fetters for the binding of their limbs in slavery. So should it be with Bluestring's Bill. His pet scheme, which now he would fain throw aside, should be fastened like a stone about his neck—to drown him.

When Barbara drew the attention of Medlicote to the behaviour of his flame, his vanity was mortified. Of course there are as good fish to be found in the sea as ever came out of it, and Mrs. Belfield at best was not a prize one. Some day, he had carelessly reflected, it might suit him to take home the worldling as a useful piece of furniture, or select another of the same species. There was no hurry about it. But suddenly to find a rival preferred put a different face on the matter; one, too, who was by no means remarkable, or well set-off by the adornments of false hair or wired coat-skirts.

Such a proceeding puts a man upon his mettle, and Ranulph began seriously to consider what he ought to do. Pamela would suit him, of that he was quite certain; yet she was not worth a violent struggle. But to think of the penniless Scotch dreamer being placed in the esteem of any woman before Ranulph Medlicote, Esq.!

This rankled, and the Vice-Chamberlain had half

a mind to lay serious siege to the bedchamber-woman, if only to oust the presumptuous Forfar. Or would it be better at once to resign the prize with a bow and congratulations? If he chose to put forth his strength, Ranulph had no doubt of success; but was it really worth while, except for the punishment of the Jacobite, to put forth strength at all?

All things considered, Mr. Medlicote resolved for the present to be cold and reserved; for women are shifty things, and the difficulties of the moment were sufficiently grave to demand undivided attention. Yes, women, save as ornaments, are unsatisfactory creations, Ranulph assured himself. Look at this very Barbara, this sprig of quality, whom folks chose to consider charming! She was a strange mixture, not improved by her new social status. Fancy any man in his senses marrying such a girl!

Ranulph laughed aloud at the very idea. Not but what she was decorative, and would look well arrayed in jewels. But what a cypher must her husband be! If ever woman needed control she did, too fond as she clearly was of cards and improper excitement. What a tawdry set of friends she had gathered round her since she left the stage! A crew of demireps and fops and gamblers! She was cut-out for the luridly brilliant career of a stage-player. 'Twas a pity to have taken her into the uncongenial atmosphere of polite private life at all, for she showed signs of out-heroding Herod. The *rôle* of such a woman, he sagely reflected, is to shine and glitter, to be the central figure in a brilliant *entourage*, where public men like Walpole and himself could find temporary surcease from humdrum worries. Placed as she now was, she could not shine, and, despite beauty and talents, might very probably join the lengthy procession of ladies who are labelled *femmes manquées*.

This was Medlicote's deliberate opinion with regard to Mrs. Philpot, and he was not stupid. It was also the opinion of many others, who therein wronged the Diva.

No doubt many women—and many men too—are unable to appear at their best, except in a peculiar setting. Barbara knew too well that in all respects she was unsuited to the present phase of her existence. It is nonsense to say that a woman can stand alone. When she attempts to do so she invariably becomes objectionable—a *lusus naturæ*, who should be placed in a glass case as an ugly curiosity.

'Twas not strength of character that Bab required, for whatever she attempted was attacked with vigour and determination. And yet from the first she had pined for a support that was never forthcoming. As the female parent had proved a broken reed, so had the male one. In dreaming of an ideal father (so unideal a mother under her gaze), she had always seen a man, upright, stalwart, noble-browed; and 'twas a grievous deception to discover in the newly found one a pantaloon, who wished the world to suppose his mind engrossed with hair-powder and velvet.

'Twas no satisfaction to be told by partial friends that under paint and periwig there was an intellect. If there, it was of no use to her. She had never seen any of its flashes, and having naught to rest eyes on but the paint and the periwig, may be excused for disbelieving the partial ones. Hence she was thrown back upon herself—most dangerous condition for a flattered woman—without the assistance which before had served in some sort as ballast. No more wreaths, and plaudits, and engrossing daily occupation. No more struggling (in futile fashion, as she too well knew) to embody the creations of the poets. No more carping with Cibber, or lectures from Wilks. Look at it from whatever side she would, her life was unutterably dreary, and bade fair soon to be intolerable. There was no blinking the unwelcome fact that home in the Belfield *ménage* meant existence in a whited sepulchre with uncomely bones to play with.

As a toy-shop wench she had ardently desired to be a fine lady. Her desire was gratified. But fine-ladyism meant for her a purse generally empty, sordid shifts and turns from which her soul recoiled.

All this had vaguely come home to her some time since, and she had resolved, as we have seen, to seek refuge in politics. But even here untoward Fate pursued. Politicians, particularly old ones, dearly love a kind of Portia-Hypatia—a very pretty and sparkling counsellor, who lays down the law and disentangles knots in a trice which puzzle a whole cabinet of wiseacres.

There is something delicious in artless feminine assurance. When stately Helen appeared at the gate before Priam and his greybeards, did they not all agree that for the sweet sake of so lovely a vision they were prepared to endure to the uttermost?

Now, much as Bab loved dominion, she could not bring herself to prattle wisdom to old men while they sat leering at her. Politics demand an apprenticeship; for to a neophyte they are made of the mean and the *mesquin*.

In the House, old men, of gentle birth, reputed wise, descend to the vulgarest of personality and backbiting; quibble over contemptible trifles till perspiration runs down their faces; abuse each other under cover of language which they are pleased to call Parliamentary courtesy, in such fashion as among ignorant schoolboys would very properly produce trouncings and fisticuffs.

If the stage and its surroundings appeared low to Bab, the amenities of St. Stephen's were scarcely more dignified; and while with startled eyes she perceived the exceeding smallness of 'great men,' she wondered where, in its Godlike form, human nature might be found.

It would not do, she told herself in dismay, to see

so plainly the littleness of this world of ours. We must needs make the best of it, but the process grows more difficult as disillusion follows disillusion; as one by one our garments are taken from us, and we stand naked, shivering.

Leering greybeards, who behaved no better than schoolboys, were altogether distasteful to unsophisticated Bab. Lord Forfar was impossible—a natural enemy. Her only sheet-anchor was Walpole. 'Twixt herself and Sir Robert there was a father-and-daughterly feeling—result of years—which came to her as an only solace. Striving to forget herself in him, she chattered of affairs, and discussed the ins and outs of the difficult question of Excise.

The faithful henchman, Medlicote, frequently was of the party when grave matters were under discussion, and, studying her loveliness, suggested one morning that, if she chose, she might become a genuinely useful ally instead of a pretty talker. With time and skill the resentment even of a Pulteney might be disarmed by beauty. An intriguing political Delilah! Her face fell, and her pride tingled. Perhaps Mr. Ranulph would wish her to make love to Bolingbroke, the bedizened Iscariot?

Here again did the falseness of her position obtrude itself. Wedded to a man of mark, she might have bloomed into a political divinity; have queened it in her *salon* over a crowd in stars and ribbons; have done good work for the Whigs in capacity of high-born siren. But as an ex-actress, illegitimate child of Fop Belvedere, sister of Mrs. Belfield—no, the task was too difficult.

Unable to soar, she must be content with trivial things. Such small efforts as she was fitted for she would make in aid of Walpole. Their pigmy proportions were harrowing to a proud and lofty soul. Hence was it that out of sheer bitterness of spirit she took refuge in cards and routs, and the whirl of modish dissipation.

The occult power of beauty is mighty fine as exerted over knights in the lists. With the rabble 'tis not precisely the same; and my Lord Belvedere had occasion again to rebuke his offspring.

Resolved to sally out one afternoon in the direction of Westminster with the intention of addressing certain mob-leaders on the vexed question of the hour, Mrs. Philpot arrayed herself in a bewitching costume and ordered her booby-hutch—a neatly turned-out vehicle, which was Byron's last gift ere she became a 'sprig.'

But she was no sooner on the ground than the advanced guard of the malcontents, perceiving the Whig colours fluttering from horses and postilion, made a roaring rush and demolished the pony-chaise, placing its owner in some little peril. This was disconcerting and offensive.

'Cymon and Iphigenia, forsooth!' she muttered, while gazing on the ruin. 'Like most other legends, 'tis a cheat. The brazen creature, we know, had nothing on. Had she worn a sacque of the Whig colours, for instance, much conquest she would have made of Cymon!'

Alas! In no sense of the word, as she plainly told herself, was the erst too victorious Barbara a trump card now. The philanderers were not at ease, as in the jolly days when they could hover and swear and spit unchecked about the staircase of the Lock of Hair.

Then 'twas understood that she was the one unchallenged idol on the premises, before whose altar worshippers might deposit anything, secure of smiles. Now it was otherwise. The possible advent of perfumed my lord was discomfiting; the whiskings of the Honourable Pamela more so. Besides, it becomes fine-ladyism to cultivate fine ladies.

Ranulph was right about Bab's friends. The female ones were past-mistresses of the college of scandal and modish wickedness, whose pointed raillery disconcerted those gentlemen who were there to adore the one.

The three Miss Mostyns, for example, to whom prim Gervas took such exception, were fop-scramblers by profession, who laughed at everything honest as nauseous cant; who, true to their colours of bubble, juggle, and chicane, wore vizards as commonly as gloves; made up for the night in masks of oilskin, larded with cat-marrow, hare's gall and ground hogs' bones; were too fond of substituting for the Chinese leaf at the tea-table aniseed, cinnamon, Barbadoes water, and orange brandy. Not good friends, these, for a girl in a difficult position!

In quiet moments her reflections being of a grim order, the troublous days that passed during the Excise suspense came in guise of a relief.

Bab saw the possibility of playing mouse to Walpole's lion, and burned for an early chance of displaying her usefulness. On both sides champions were wary, eying each other's motions with drawn sabres.

Having accurately taken the measure of a dear sister, and being on the *qui vive*, she thought it rather odd when, one day at the palace, the Honourable Pamela was good enough to be affectionate.

Since she, Pamela, that gushing maiden said, was compelled by a never-too-much-to-be-regretted slavery to lodge in the palace, why did not dear Barbara soften evening solitude by giving little parties? 'Twould amuse my lord, their father, who, odsheartikins, regretted youth and bachelorhood. Not the Mostyns, nor Byron, nor that nasty old satyr, Mr. Ambassador Hastang. Naughty Barbara, to cultivate such comrades! Something more serious and decorous, calculated to entertain the better part of my lord, their parent. Alack-a-day! she, Pamela, was unfortunate in being attached

to the wrong side. Her friends did not find favour
with papa; but Barbara's would. Why not—happy
idea—give little suppers after the House was up?
Walpole and that brainless importunate coxcomb
Medlicote were friends of Barbara's and of her
papa. Of course the poor bedchamber drudge would
have no part in the pleasant gatherings, but in the
midst of drudgery 'twould be too delicious for Pam
to reflect upon the happy lot of others.

Barbara, although suspicious and awake, seeing
no harm, innocently and promptly adopted the idea,
marvelling the while what Pamela's motive could be.
The more she revolved the suggestion the more
mystified did she become. That Mrs. Belfield was
the last maiden in the world weakly to succumb to
paltry good-nature she knew. What could be her
object? 'Twas worth studying.

Meanwhile the wretched Walpole did need
sympathy. Soon 'twould be imperatively needful
to call out the military for his own personal defence.
Going in and out of the House he was hustled,
hissed, hooted, spit upon; was forced sometimes to
escape through my Lord Halifax's lodgings.

Opposition, warned of his intent, declined to allow
the obnoxious Bill quietly to be dropped. No! They
vowed so wicked an attack on British liberties ought
to be stigmatized by every possible mark of emphatic
opprobrium—its evil-minded pioneer to be well
pummelled.

There was to be a demonstration in Parliament and out—the nose of the base Minister was to be rubbed in the dirt-pie that he had made. He would be sore harassed, have much to bear.

Bab, seeking in vain for a harmful motive on her sister's part, adopted her suggestion. The ordeal of the fateful night well over, he and his tiny knot of faithful ones were to be entertained at supper by their 'little Whig.'

My Lord Belvedere, wily as usual, did not disapprove. He would absent himself. If all went well he would point to the fact of the entertainment having taken place at his house; if ill, he would swear he knew nothing of it, or why not have been there himself?

Bolingbroke had taken his measures craftily. Though the fate of Excise was practically sealed, there was more howling at the funeral than at the birth. Lobbies, Court of Requests, open spaces, coigns of vantage, were crowded by a yelling rabble in his pay; and Walpole, as, with hat unlooped and roquelaure draped over nose and chin, he slunk into St. Stephen's, accompanied by Crump, muttered that so intimidating an element at the very threshold of the House was more destructive to the independence of the Commons than any corrupt pecuniary court influence which he had ever brought to bear.

Westminster Hall resembled Drury, for Whigs and Tories had gathered their forces there, and the knights of the shoulder-knot, with sturdy calves and brawny shoulders, were as threatening and unruly as they had ever been on the first representation of a comedy.

My Lord Bolingbroke was severely blamed for fomenting a scandal within the venerable precincts; 'twas just like his malice, Members said, to fling mud into the temple whose doors were closed to him. Not that the footmen's turbulence would have proved serious but for after-consequences. True, they used their silver-tipped staves with good effect, and set much honest claret running; but phlebotomy is useful oftentimes for the purging of humours. They hustled the members of rival sides, protected their masters' friends, heartily banged each other's sconces for several hours; then moved to the two mug-houses opposite, to spend each man the crown he had earned in such toasts as he deemed appropriate.

Now one of these mug-houses over against St. Stephen's bore the sign of the Walpole's Head; and to it on the memorable evening that was to see the final struggle moved a goodly deputation from the Loyal Society of the Roebuck, whose headquarters, as all the world knows, is in Cheapside. Even the roughest and bluntest Britons love fair play, and Mr. Crump, resolved that the Dawley party should not have disorder to themselves, sent down to the Roebuck to complain of browbeating.

The Jacobites, he declared, were bent on destroying the Protestant Succession, and condemning a devoted metropolis to the use of wooden shoes. His patron, he averred, had abandoned Excise—there was no question of it any more. Having bowed to popular will, would they, loyal Protestants, see him gagged and maltreated by a set of malignant Torquemadas?

The Loyal Society answered the appeal with three cheers, and sallied out in force for the scene of action with the emblems and effigies which they kept always ready—namely, the Pope, the Pretender, and the Devil, done to the life in straw; and a warming-pan and a sucking-bottle to boot, dangling as standard from a pole.

On their way they made a raid on grocers' shops for links, and by the time they reached Westminster presented the formidable aspect of a fiery snake.

My Lord Bolingbroke intended to coerce the Ministry? Oh, indeed! Protestants could demonstrate quite as well as he. In front of the Walpole's Head they would burn their effigies, and if loyal cits did not provide beer and gin for those who danced around, England was no longer what she was.

But the Anti-Excise party, perceiving the fiery line with its three wagging figure-heads, determined not to be outdone. Outside the other mug-house on t'other side o' the road they would burn their figures —the fat man and the fat woman—with quite as loud huzzas; and the swarming mob within the precincts of the yard, hearing of the rival armies, poured forth in force to take part in the fun. Bricks and stones flew like hail, and the sight of many lying bleeding on the pavement roused the spirit of the rest to serious warfare.

Mr. Crump, who gazed out of a window, began to wonder whether he had been right. 'Twas certainly outrageous that the Dawleyites should have it their own way. If his patron was compelled to eat humble pie within-doors, 'twas well that his party should be victorious without; and Honest Jack was pleased to perceive that the Loyal Society were in force, and likely to gain the mastery.

As he looked, the rolling snowball increased and gathered till he wist not which party was the stronger; for, verily, from the slums of Tothillfields and Waterside there flocked, like vultures to the carcase, a horde of the ragged and unwashed, who cared only for mischief and drink and booty.

There was a muster of dissolute Bridewell prentices, and a gang of weavers from Spitalfields, who for some time had been wanted by the justices for flinging pernicious fluids at wearers of foreign silk.

Then there arose as from the earth a *posse* of discharged sailors, armed with short bludgeons; and soon after—ill news spreads fast—a contingent of butchers from St. James's Market, who long had been the natural foes of the valets and footmen of that quarter. Elements of a very pretty disturbance, in good sooth; beholding which, Honest Jack was filled with satisfaction. For with such a boiling of the caldron in the open air, Members on both sides would be cowed, and anxious to adjourn the sitting.

But, as he looked, satisfaction changed to curses. Maladroit marplots! why interfere? Sure it mattered not how many of such pates were broken, and the diversion so artfully caused would be most salutary. But some blundering magistrate must needs meddle—was standing on a horseblock reading the Riot Act. Well done! over he tumbled, heels in air, and the human waters covered him. Bungling fool and idiot, serve him right if he were crushed!

Out came the footmen from either mug-house—swarm of parti-coloured bees—and the *mêlée* became general, surging in and out, up the intervening street and back. A nimble Bridewell lad was up the post. Down toppled Walpole's head.

That was bad! But the Loyal Society would avenge the insult. Yes. A spark, a sheet of flame—the Pope, the Pretender, and the Devil were burning bravely; but, alack! so also were the fat man and woman. The image of her gracious Majesty, indeed, spluttered with a salvo of crackers, which called forth a ringing cheer.

Suddenly the wheeling circles wavered and fell back—for an instant. The space about the twin fires was bare. Something must be coming down the narrow street invisible to the spectator at the window.

Ah! the long white leggings and tall caps adorned with the horse of Hanover! An ensign and a hundred men of the 3rd Regiment of Footguards. What a pity! Whatever befell, the odium of calling out the military would fall on Walpole; and the sight of the white cross-belts and gaiters was sure to exasperate the populace.

The sailors, reckless, storm-beaten fellows, were the first to rally; then, with loud acclaim and a shower of missiles, butchers and footmen, forgetting private feud, made common cause against the soldiers. Pope, Pretender, Devil, fat man and woman were forgot, and, only half-consumed, were trampled under foot, the fires scattered. Bayonets glittered in the yellow torchlight; the ensign was seen to bare his head and gesticulate. Then came a shower of mud and stones; soldiers and sailors closed and locked, swayed to and fro. The first row of tall hats garnished with the pale horse broke their line, mingled with the blue-coats, and went down. The second advanced at a trot. A puff of smoke—a rattle of musketry! Good heavens, how rash! They had fired on the people!

Mr. Crump rushed down the stairs in a fluster, and across the open to St. Stephen's.

The street and alleys were cleared. The sailors,

with a low growl like the beating of their own salt sea, fell, chafing, back.

'For God's sake, fire no more!' cried Crump, panting, as he ran past.

The tall-hats formed in square and stood at ease. Three men were lying dead; a dozen, or more, were writhing in their blood. The mob looked one at another, irresolute, but fierce; and with the sailors, who had led the fray, withdrew slowly, bearing their wounded within the barrier which protected the entrance to the House.

'Twas a grievous misadventure. If only the rioters had been left to settle their differences all would have been well. As his secretary ascended the stair Sir Robert and his party were descending, and Crump, explaining rapidly what had chanced, implored his patron to depart some other way. But Walpole was at bay.

'What!' he cried, with indignation, to his son Edward and Medlicote, who walked on either side. 'There hath been too much of flight. If I run away they'll think me guilty of this deplorable mistake— I, who knew nought of it. Forward, gentlemen! stick close.'

A small negro boy, with glittering eyes and flashing teeth, sped across the open, and up the stairs, and, breathless, handed to Medlicote a billet.

'Strange!' he muttered, glancing over the contents. 'From Mrs. Philpot! 'Tis well. Behind us, child, or thou'lt be swept out of existence.'

As Crump feared, the sight of Sir Robert roused the mob to madness. The soldiery being at a safe distance, their weltering victims called for vengeance. With a wild yell of execration they dashed across the marble lobby and made for the Minister; but both friends and political foes formed a cohort around him, while a body of forty or fifty constables in red waistcoats, emerging from the House, battled to form a lane.

Lord Forfar, dropping for once his melancholy calm, stood forth with Pulteney and strove to appease the press. Whatever their plans might be with regard to Walpole, they had no desire to see him murdered. Mr. Crump's broad shoulders stood him in good stead as he and Ranulph, forgetful of his smart clothes, drew their swords and moved down in front of their patron.

Some blew out the lamps. What a jostling and struggling in the dark narrow stairwell! Would none warn the soldiery without of the tragedy that was passing within earshot?

'Keep your feet, gentlemen!' cried Walpole, above the din, 'for he who falls will never rise again.'

The click of swords, the thud of sticks and staves formed fit accompaniment to the hard-breathing, the hissing of oaths and execrations through set teeth. Some miscreant behind, taking his hint, strove to trip Sir Robert, who, being bulky, would have faired ill indeed had not his son and General Churchill held him erect. Another, seizing his red roquelaure, strove to strangle him; but luckily the strings broke, and the gurgling Minister for the time was saved.

The scuffle lasted but a moment, for the soldiers, so soon as they were aware of what passed, advanced at the double with fixed bayonets, and the avenging flood, attacked in front and rear, parted like water, melted and ebbed away.

Edward Walpole, Crump, and Ranulph, supporting Sir Robert, who, unused to personal violence, was purple in the face and could scarce stand, hurried him away, and finding a coach, got into it.

'To St. James's,' Ranulph said. 'Your pay according to your speed.'

But Sir Robert, as soon as he could speak, gasped:

'Not so! We are engaged to Bab. My wig's in ribbons and so's my coat; I've lost my watch and my star—happily 'twas a steel and not my diamond one. The danger's past; methinks we've earned our supper.'

'While seeming unfortunate, luck favours us,' responded Ranulph. 'See! another minute and I should have missed this note, which appears of gravest import.'

By light of passing lamps he read aloud :

'" Most urgent. Avoid our street as ye would jail-fever. Supper in your chambers.—BAB."'

' Whatever can she mean, the madcap !' pondered Sir Robert, as bareskulled he examined his wrecked periwig. '" Most urgent " ! Hath the night yet other surprises in store ? Well, we shall soon know.' With which sapient conclusion the exhausted Minister lay back in the coach, feeling his injured throat and marvelling exceedingly.

Without further mishap the party reached the palace, and, having determined that their Majesties must be told nothing till the morrow, or they would ask a thousand questions and chatter till sunrise, stole quietly in by the side postern, of which Ranulph held a key, and which communicated directly with his apartments.

A-tiptoe, like burglars, they reached the chambers of the Vice-Chamberlain, at the foot of the Queen's private stair. Oh, charming audacity! On entering they found all the candles alight, and the board spread with flowers and appetizing delicacies, while Mrs. Philpot, clad in the sweetest waiting-wench's garb, tripped hither and thither arranging knives and platters.

The aspect of the banquet and the comely array of right claret in cut decanters smoothed the last wrinkles of Sir Robert's anxiety.

' What is this prank of our little Whig's ?' he

cried, rubbing his palms cheerily. 'Mrs. Clive would die of envy if she saw that chambermaid's attire. I vow I'm hungry as a bumbailiff!'

'Then all hath gone well?' inquired Bab. 'I borrowed my dress of my own woman, who hath a *tendre* for your man, Mr. Medlicote, and procured us entrance without trouble through yonder private passage in the postern. There's method in this masquerading. At every crack of this old woodwork my heart has been in my mouth for your sake—but, good lack! A *posse* of ragamuffins! Blood! Mr. Medlicote, you are hurt? What hath befallen?'

Ranulph, in truth, had received a nasty cut in the dark scrimmage, which, though not dangerous, bled freely; and Mr. Crump ground his teeth with envy when he contemplated the solicitude of Barbara as with light woman's fingers she staunched and tied it up.

Oh! to feel those fingers upon his breast; to mark the transient paleness; the breath quickened on his account through those parted cherry lips! How gladly would he have endured a far more serious wound to be thus tended! Concerning him and how he had fared she never asked. His clothes were in tatters, though his skin was whole. Oh! the jocund ripple of those silver bells as, observing Sir Robert's torn shirt and moulting periwig, she broke into a shout of irreverent laughter. But she should be his yet. He had sworn it. When would the day arrive?

As she was briefly informed of what had passed, Bab became thoughtful; and, having heard, proceeded in turn to relate her own adventures. Still waters run deep. Who would have thought that the lofty and superior Lord Forfar would condescend to the use of the very dirtiest weapons? 'Twas whimsical and entertaining, now that peril was averted. Though a Jacobite, Gervas was a Protestant, and therefore had no right to act on the Jesuit principle. Yet 'twas from his brain, as it appeared, that had emanated the notable scheme which she had been permitted by fortune to frustrate. Her prayer had been heard. The mouse had been allowed to help the lion. She, Barbara Philpot, had undone the evil unwittingly wrought with regard to the £1,000; had repaid the sum in kind. She and her friend were quits.

Whilst consenting to act upon the suggestion dropped by Pamela, she continued to wonder over that young lady's object, and, uneasy, was alert. Arrangements for the little festival being complete, she was sitting by the open window watching the slow lighters, as, letting down the swing-ropes which supported the street-lamps, they filled them with oil, ignited a glowworm glimmer, and hauled them back into their places. What with increasing lawlessness, and what with the public interest being turned in the direction of Westminster, street and park were a desert.

Suspicious already, she was startled to perceive a group of men in the Park walk, whose numbers increased by additions of one or two till there was a goodly handful. Presently they entered the street by the green wicket, and strolled past the house, talking in husky whispers. She recognised them. They were myrmidons of Mr. Figg—bruisers of the lower sort, whom she had often seen at the Bearpit, or sparring at May Fair! What in the name of Lucifer could their object be, sauntering in the modish quarter?

At first she thought 'twas some new freak of my Lord Byron's (here Crump blushed scarlet, and lowered his eyes upon his supper), till she reflected that though that *vaurien* might carry off a player or a dancer, he would not dare to lay violent hands upon a sprig of quality. Bruisers, too! Something important must be in the wind; and it suddenly flashed across the little Whig that their presence and the sisterly hint might possibly be connected. Waiting for an entertainment that might not take place till the small hours was not amusing. Why not kill time by a frolic which might perchance end in a discovery?

Ringing for her abigail, Mrs. Philpot borrowed a suit of her garments ('The most becoming of suits,' suggested Mr. Crump) and the two girls in apron, coif and cardinal, strolled forth to admire the evening, guilelessly arm-in-arm. At the first turn sundry of the broken-nosed fraternity winked and grinned, displaying great tusks. At the second they offered a polite ' How do ye ?' with elephantine compliment anent waists and ankles. At the third, one took Mrs. Philpot in his paw and inflicted a great smack upon her lips (here Mr. Crump choked, and had to be smitten on his broad back), in return for which he got another smack—a tingling one upon the ear (here Mr. Crump grew better).

The ice thus genially broken, the twin serving-maids—arms akimbo, noses tilted, ankles well displayed—assailed and routed the enemy, who fled in confusion.

'They ran down the street?' inquired approving Crump.

'No, fool!' retorted Barbara; ''twas woman's warfare, a pointed tongue the rapier. They buffeted like elephants and tumbled us, but we wormed out what we wanted in a trice, and we twisted our bodies out of their bears' paws. They were waiting for no woman, but a man, they admitted. A revelation! What manner of man I cared not to inquire—for there could be but one—the noblest, best of burly gentlemen, in a snuffy coat and a blue ribbon!'

Tears of joy rose into Bab's eyes, as, stretching across the table, she clasped Sir Robert's hand.

'Motioning to my abigail, we withdrew from the

contest. I sent a hurried message to Mr. Medlicote by my black boy, while we two came staggering out presently with a great basket, cursing the whimsies of the quality. The gladiators of the Bearpit were for recommencing hostilities' (here a piece of Mr. Crump's pie again went the wrong way), 'but we disdainfully informed them that if they had duties, so had we. If they were men-catchers we were housewives, and must even drag our linen to the wash by the strength of our women's arms.'

Barbara's tale, embellished with piquant mimickry and byplay, was a tremendous histrionic triumph. She had missed her vocation, Ranulph swore. No doubt her Lady Townly and Lady Betty Modish were beyond compare; but her Lettice or Miss Prue would be ravishing! Would she deign to return to the boards for one week, if only to be the death of Madam Clive? The eyes of Crump were so full of hot meaning that Barbara coloured and looked down.

'Well, one might be living on the coast of Barbary!' grunted Sir Robert. 'Attempted murder in the House of Commons, kidnapping in St. James's! And this is our boasted civilization!'

One thing was evident. The tact and wit of the ex-Diva had saved the Minister from serious personal peril. He rose upon his gouty legs, which ached no little after recent occurrences, and said that he felt one bounden duty, and that was to drink the health, with hearty love and thankfulness, of the beauteous creature whom he was happy and proud to call his guardian angel.

'Here's to my little Whig: God bless her!' he said, with faltering accents; and as he looked across his brimming glass, his eyes and hers were brimming also.

In sooth 'twas an affecting moment: all felt it so, as, touching glass-rims and forgetting where they were, the party shouted aloud the toast of 'Barbara Philpot!'

The shout ran through the low, wainscoted room, and passing up the spiral stair reached the astonished ear of Mrs. Belfield, who was on duty in the chamber of her Majesty.

Barbara Philpot! What whiff was this of the hated presence which assaulted her hearing even in princely St. James's, in the small hours? She must have nodded, and been dreaming! A nightmare? Yet, no! Her nerves and ambition were on the twitter, her blood too feverish for sleep, as, lounging in an elbow-chair, still dressed, she wondered what had chanced at home.

There had been no news. Could the House be sitting still? It must be so, or Medlicote would have intruded on the royal slumbers, knowing the anxiety of Caroline for news. Perchance they would sit all night.

What then of the salt prepared for the bird's tail?

She knew that Bab had fallen into the trap; had unwittingly become the snare to catch the Minister. She had received the thanks of both Forfar and Pulteney, who had prepared their gin.

Pulteney had been profuse of compliment; Forfar had looked into her eyes with the expression that she wished; had whispered that James III. would himself thank her. Where was Walpole now? If the House sat till the morrow, for the time he would be saved; for even amid the rioting 'twould be impossible by day to lay violent hands on the First Minister.

What then? Was the building she was erecting made of cards, to be blown down by the breath of accident? No, surely; for by general consent the Excise Bill was abandoned: there was nothing doing that could keep the House all night.

Where was Sir Robert, then? Bound hand and foot, with gag in mouth, and bandage over eyes, in a coach half-way to Gravesend? Perhaps already there, on board the vessel which was to sail with him across the ocean. No! That could not be, for though time was slow and laggard to her who waited in suspense, the ship could not sail before the morning.

But why had Ranulph not appeared? Had he also been taken and shipped off? What if it were so? Would she be grieved? Why should she care? The die being cast for Gervas, Ranulph was a nuisance, and best away. On the whole she was rather glad that her beau suitor should have shared the fate of Walpole.

Through some such dreaming came the faint echo of 'Barbara Philpot.' What could it imply? Whence did it come? Down the chimney? Through the keyhole? From below? 'Twas no fancy, for the Queen also heard the sound, and ringing a handbell, bade the woman who watched in the ante-chamber to go down and make inquiries.

A sickening dread of she knew not what calamity tightened the bosom of Mrs. Belfield. She would go herself and see. With both hands clasped upon her breast she sped down the winding stair, and staggering, stopped with cold fingers on the door-handle, which unconsciously she turned.

What a sight met her view! A dazzle of mellow radiance; a table sumptuously spread; a party of gentlemen, mud and blood stained, holding glasses aloft; at the end one woman seated, whose flushed cheek was moist with happy tears.

Standing there, Pamela could have shrieked and shaken fists at Heaven like a Mænad, but for the sparkle of those mocking eyes that scoffed at her. Barbara knew all—'twas evident by the insulting smile which slowly spread over her face, as, rising and curtseying low, she demurely pointed to a seat and bade her 'sister' welcome.

Sister! Hateful word and loathsome woman!

The scheme had somehow miscarried. Walpole, little the worse (except for claret), was there in the palace; so was Ranulph and Crump and all the crew, and—and—*Barbara*!

The men were safe. How much did they know? Perhaps 'twas accident that damped the powder; prevented the explosion! What, then, did Barbara here, insultingly triumphant in her scorn? Curbing twanging nerves with a sharp twitch of the rein, Mrs. Belfield raised her brows and quietly said:

'Pardon my intrusion on an orgy. Her Majesty above hath been awakened by unseemly uproar. I will withdraw and tell her of the cause.'

Both Sir Robert and Ranulph looked somewhat sheepish, as schoolboys might, detected supping in the dormitory. How stupid to have forgotten that the Queen's couch was overhead, and that if awake she must be half delirious with curiosity!

Pamela was prim and cold, a perambulating wet-blanket, chill enough to quench the ardour of the most jovial. Therefore Sir Robert, generally too prone to be gallant, had always treated the bed-chamber-woman with an indifference which was accentuated outrage.

Now he hated her. Somebody must go to the Queen. Ranulph was accustomed to talk to his august mistress through a door-chink. Once more must the faithful henchman sacrifice himself.

In obedience to a look, Mr. Medlicote sighed and

slowly mounted the staircase, rather admiring his lady-love than otherwise for the fine breeding of her unsurprised severity.

'Twas feminine jealousy of another woman that caused Bab to drop hints of Pamela's connection with the kidnapping. That she should be so connected was on the face of it most improbable.

Yet there must be a clear understanding, if ever he came to propose marriage, that she was not to coquet with the Pretender. Marriage! 'Twould be a folly, and unnecessary follies in such ticklish times were to be deprecated. She could not really care for the stiff Jacobite. No. 'Twas Barbara's mischief. The malicious puss! As he departed he heard her say with mock solemnity:

'There are roaring lions, my dear, in our street, seeking whom they may devour. Helpless maidens are in danger there, so I've come to sleep with you!'

CHAPTER IV.

A THIEVES' HOLIDAY.

ALTHOUGH the firing of the volley by the King's Footguards was in itself a regrettable circumstance, Walpole was not slow to perceive that capital was to be made out of it. Excise was dead and buried—the favourite bantling was strangled in its birth. The memory thereof had to be forgotten, and the tables turned upon the foe.

Instructed by his chief, Mr. Ranulph Medlicote was glib at the coffee-houses anent deep-laid schemes for assassination as well as kidnapping. Like other men of figure, so soon as he was dressed he was in the habit of taking a plain chair and going the round of the houses, which at noon are always crowded by the *beau monde*, a mart for gossip and tattle.

The circle can be made in an hour. Bachelors pay a guinea a week for their 'morning chair,' employing the men at other times as messengers. Then in fine weather they stroll in the Park till two; if wet, move to basset at White's, or to politics at the British, according to their views and inclinations. Of course a Tory could not be seen at the St. James's, any more than a Whig at the Cocoa-tree; but the Smyrna is a debatable land where all may meet and chat. So also is Mrs. Rochford's.

At three o'clock comes dinner. The best ordinary for strangers is in Suffolk Street; but the usual plan is to make up a party at the coffee-house, and adjourn thence to a tavern, unless you choose to go to the table of some great personage who keeps open house. There are not so many of these as there used to be, for the Revolution has impoverished the grandees. Some, however (on the Roman principle of 'clients'), manage to dine free all the year round, having fourteen great mansions on their list, using each once a fortnight.

At five or six comes the play, and after that, men of quality adjourn to Tom's or Will's till midnight, or play cards in ladies' drawing-rooms.

Ranulph made himself very busy, and so did Mr. Crump, who was not to be outdone in devotion.

'If absolute monarchy is tyranny,' sententiously remarked that sage to a gaping throng, 'absolute democracy means mob-law, which is tyranny and anarchy as well.' Adding that there had been mistakes on both sides, and that it behoved the children of Britain, like those of Noah, to veil the shortcomings of their parent.

Walpole, for his part, was convinced that he had not bribed sufficiently, and resolved in the future to be more liberal. The Jacobites for a moment had been almost united. This was very wrong, and must never be allowed again to happen. As for outcry, he shrugged his shoulders at it. Gabble-gabble! The short-sighted and the narrow-souled are like narrow-necked bottles—the less there is within, the more noise the stuff makes in coming out. He must be content, if necessary, to bide his time, certain that the world's progress, if slow, is steady—that the tide moves ever in the direction of liberty, ebbing now and again, but always towards freedom and light.

Despite the lectures to which he perforce submitted, he grew cheerful and serene, observing in his jocose way, that as coarse mothers have comely children, so might Anarchy, past and done with, be the father of a settled Government. One thing he had learnt by recent events, and that was that the Pretender was more dangerous a bugbear than he had chosen to suppose; for if James II. was a mole and a blind bigot, the Chevalier was aware that he could not reintroduce Popery without hazarding the Crown. Hence, many Protestants who, for religion's sake, had deserted the old house, had shown themselves not unwilling to support it again, provided the faith was secure.

This grave fact had become patent to Sir Robert by the manner in which he had found himself thrown over during the late fiasco. Another thing had forced itself on the attention of the Minister as he watched the development of the riot—the exceeding depravity and drunkenness of the lower orders, and their growing partiality for gin.

Now, to good honest beer Sir Robert was too thoroughly English to object. Beer-drinkers are good-humoured in their cups. The ill-effect of the love of gin was remarked by all shrewd observers. It degraded the physique as well as the intelligence. Men and women withered to skeletons, and in their hollow eyes there lurked the lambent flame of fierce and savage vice.

A Member of Parliament, Sir Joseph Jekyll, drew the attention of Sir Robert to the matter in the first instance, and suggested that an Act should be passed prohibiting the sale of what was well named 'Blue Ruin.' Walpole quite agreed with Sir Joseph, but demurred as to the means to be adopted. When coercive legislation is commenced, 'tis so difficult to draw a line; and yet there was no doubt that the matter required attention.

'Are Englishmen turned cowards,' he asked of his little Whig, 'that during the recent troubles the use of the knife hath grown so common? When I was young fists were good enough; now London cits sit paralyzed while miscreants set fire to their houses, every muscle relaxed, every nerve shuddering in the hour of danger. Sure this should be altered at any cost or risk.'

'Twas all very well for Bab to tilt her pretty nose and shake a warning finger. This proposed Act was necessary; and he would go with her to Southwark Fair that she might judge of the truth of his words.

'I am aware,' he said, somewhat dolefully, 'that we are rickety things of straw, liable to overturn. Who should know it, if not I? But we have our use in the world's economy, and must be content to struggle on, warding off as many buffets as we may.'

'Don't be miserable,' rejoined the sapient counsellor, 'or I shall cry, and that will spoil my beauty. A scarecrow is stuffed with straw, you know, and yet 'tis vastly useful to protect the corn. Of course we'll go to Southwark; but I won't have that plotting Scotchman of the party, as arranged. He's too deep and artful. Make piles of Acts, as a wise statesman should; but before passing unnecessary ones condescend to consider your own immediate wants, and prop up your rickety strawship.'

The arch maiden was right. Was she not always right? So had been her sharp-witted Grace of

Queensberry when she warned him long ago not to despise his enemies. Well, they should plot against him with impunity no more. Just fancy! but for the little Whig he might have been ere this half-way to Barbadoes!

The big broom was brought out of the loft, and great was the sweeping in the stable. Dismay and consternation spread among the mutineers. Chesterfield, Clinton, Grafton, and ever so many more, were flung out like so much lumber. Hitherto 'twas only the aspiring who received hard measure at the hands of the good-natured Walpole—but now he had turned a new leaf—the autocrat had become a tyrant. Even the despicable Grafton was worth a kick; the man of whom Swift had said that 'he was a slobberer without one good quality!'

The chagrin of my Lord Bolingbroke at these smart measures can be imagined. Its depth was made manifest to the Dawley coterie by the growing rigidity of his indifference. Again the red shoes paraded between the furrows, but with an increased following; for of course the ejected malcontents now openly joined his side, and howled behind the farmer in chorus.

'Walpole hath cut me dead!' announced Gervas, with a whimsical tinge of surprise, as he dismounted one morning at the farm-gate. 'Her Grace of Queensberry hath closed her saloons since a neutral ground is no longer possible, and maketh a pretext for her retirement out of the death of her pocket-poet.'

So the toady was defunct—the may-fly. My Lord Forfar wronged her Grace, for she was genuinely sorry over the demise of Mr. Gay, who died at Burlington Gardens, aged forty-six.

'The world is a pitiful thing,' she writ to Swift. 'Not only doth it perform no promise for the future, but every day annuls the meagre pleasure of the past! After the first heats are over, life is all downhill; and one would wish for the journey's end if sure to lie down easy when night o'ertaketh us!'

But my Lord Bolingbroke was too bitter to trouble anent the may-fly. 'Twas terrible to feel the iron heel of that irrepressible Sir Bluestring, who, stronger than ever for the check which had cost such trouble, went blooming down the Mall with the open declaration that he could seduce any whom he had a mind to gain, and crush the others like an egg!

Oh, the clumsy, impertinent, spoiled child of fickle Fortune, who, undermining by fraud his native land, could call the process *governing!* Oh, the depraved, degraded nobility, who, reduced by luxury and play to beg unhallowed alms, could desert their *rôle* of bulwark to cringe, wretched hirelings, and accept at such dirty hands the wages of iniquity! Really, 'twas hardly worth while to rail. Better to cultivate crops, oblivion, and peace.

'If you come to a certain humble farm in Middlesex,' writ the farmer to Pulteney, 'you will find that I can live frugally without ill-temper, and yet I've as little disposition towards frugality as any man alive! I have just risen, refreshed, serene; not jaded as I used to be in town with bootless frivolous anxiety!'

'What graver solecism can there be,' he snorted to his disciples, 'than a nobility which deliberately sells the liberty of the Commons? In aristocracies the nobles gain what the Commons lose. In monarchies the result of helping to enslave the Commons is that they themselves will be enslaved, the Crown alone the gainer! Oh, these nobles—these nobles! Men who boast the vain honour of cocking hats in the presence of princes, and yet cringe before the parasite! 'Tis poverty that is responsible for all and every evil. Our aristocracy is impoverished. Our earls have six starved footmen in gold lace behind the coach, and no wine in the cellar. Such fortunes as the South Sea and all its progeny of bubbles have left them is squandered in intrigue—in lace, knickknacks, Italian singers, and French tumblers.'

Although the ejected malcontents were rueful enough over their own undoing, they could not but smile at my Lord Bolingbroke, whose trite maxims and complainings were ladled forth, the white finger-tips of one hand poised against those of t'other, with a languid half-torpid air, and a ring of the completest insincerity. Singular that outwitted Iscariot should wear his mask so ill.

'Passions are the gales of life,' he observed mournfully to a cow that mooed at him. 'I have done with them—for ever! My friends,' he added, turning in his brocaded suit to lean on the no less elegantly caparisoned Chesterfield, who shared his rural stroll, 'let us not complain when the gales have ceased to blow a storm. What hurt doth age give us in subduing that which all our lives we are trying to subdue?'

And then the pair of actors, linked arm-in-arm, sniffing with pretended enjoyment rural scents, stifled their sighs. Pining for the pavement instead of the muddy road, they walked home with a simper of beatitude, which in both cases but half concealed intensest bitterness, the most turbid lees of black and festering disappointment.

For the present the best thing they could do was to philosophize and hope for a turn of the wheel. Hope—for what? Had not the Dawley junta just used all the armoury of craft? and had not every weapon broken in their grasp? They had paid the most scurrilous pens, employed writers who, having no consciences, fought blushless through the mire of faction; unscrupulous vipers who mangled the overthrown—whose brows were covered with the brazen frontlet of falsehood. And to what purpose?

Sir Bluestring bloomed like a great peony. As the prompter breathed the puppets squeaked! Verily, 'twas little use hoping, for the devil was out of humour. As usual he deserted his adherents at a pinch, declining to turn a vagrant attention to his own in their extremity.

Of all the personages who strove by means of stilts to keep out of low company, but whose untoward fate connected them with Southwark Fair, the one whose annual tribulation appeared most gruesome was Colley Cibber, Esq. The poet laureate! What could a gentleman so grand as he have to do with such gambadoes?

In a whisper let it be confessed that this great man—retired now to *otium cum dig.*—was once the possessor of a booth. Was a 'Bartholemew babe of grace!' Oh no! not one of the common wooden tents of iniquity! A superior booth with gilt boxes and glass lustres filled with wax candles, wherein he deigned to strut during the fourteen days of the frolic as Tamerlane, before the King and the nobility. He did not like to be reminded of it now—Colley Cibber, Esq., of Berkeley Square—and yet each year he was compelled to make the pilgrimage; for though the theatre bored him, his Majesty loved the rough humours of Bartlemy and Southwark, where he was jostled by knaves of every degree from the merry-andrew to the pickpocket. Of all the fairs, Southwark, which immediately followed Bartlemy, was the lowest and most popular. We have remarked, early in this chronicle, upon the peculiar condition of the Borough—its liberties, sanctuaries, prisons. If Bartlemy and May were lawless and dissolute carnivals, how much more so was the annual festival of Southwark, practically exempted as it was from judicial control. Colonel de Veil, terror of metropolitan evildoers, had, as I have pointed out, no authority on Surrey side. Officers of the prison-marshals and warders prowled among the crowd, gathering victims when they durst; but the seamen, broommen, Wapping beaux, and black-eyed beauties of Foul Lane were pretty sure to rush to the rescue, so the bailiffs did little service. Gangs of cutpurses from Chick Alley hustled the lieges when opportunity served, who were knocked down and trampled, while there was a raid on many watches, kerchiefs, wigs. A basket of mouldy fruit was thrown among the women who, tumbled and flustered, found themselves bereft of hoods and aprons. But this was mere horseplay; the fool who carried aught that was worth stealing, deserved his loss; 'twas local colour which added to the fascination of the scene. Not but what after-effects were sometimes serious, for City servant-maids could not be kept from the jubilee. The hopping booths were infested by handsome young land-sharks, who in the turn of a country-dance made love; and what with burnt brandy and politeness, many a maiden found herself undone, initiated into looseness and debauchery, conniver at burglary and housebreaking. By every thief the fair of Southwark was looked on as a benefit performance.

But if the picture had a shady side, it also had a bright one. Ignorant foreigners may prate of spleen, yet Englishmen in the mass are, if rough and blunt, more truly merry and good-humoured, and more forbearing than any other nation.

'Twas a just appreciation of this that caused the Prime Minister to shake his head over the new effects of gin. Had not Mr. Hogarth, the great moralist, recently preached a sermon on the subject? Thieving and drunkenness and pates honestly cracked with a cudgel were in the day's work. We can't expect perfection here below.

Pending the Gin Act, which, in spite of Barbara, he resolved to allow Jekyll to run through Parliament, he determined to shorten the periods of the fairs from fourteen to three days each, and sally forth in person to view the happy results.

As regarded himself, at Bartlemy (which chanced immediately to follow on the events related), the result was not quite pleasing; for he was battered by a mob who objected to the restrictions, and wellnigh fared as badly as at Westminster.

Mrs. Philpot was irreverent and unsympathetic, gibing at his plight.

' If you go out to get your clothes torn every day,'

she mocked, 'you'll be as great a fortune to the fop-makers as my father! If you strive to play the fool at Southwark in like fashion I'll none of your company, for my bones to me are precious.'

What was to be done about Southwark? The King, obstinate as usual, declined to renounce his trip; the Prince of Wales announced his intention to attend. 'Twould never do to risk an accident.

'How your Worship wastes a noble intellect!' laughed the young lady, who knew the spot so well. 'Do you think that the Borough, which for generations hath scorned kings and mayors, will dance now to your small pipe? Send your Lord Chamberlain, and Sergeant Trumpeter, and Mr. Crump, the Master of the Revels, and see if they're not soused in the dirtiest of all the ditches! I vow I'd like to see the condition of Honest Jack, for all his breadth of beam! No, no; Blue Ruin as yet claims no allegiance on the Surrey side; so best leave them unmolested. We drink brandy there and beer, and are the same old jovial crew of rantipoles as our grandames and grandsires were. I vow they behave no whit worse than your high-born Mohocks. If you are rational and leave them to their jolly diversions, you shall go with me. Let 'em have their way, and come under my wing, for I'm the best of ciceroni. If not, give me a wide berth, and go, tempt fortune by yourself.'

Sir Robert could not quite decide which line to

take, since his Majesty insisted upon going. He would be governed by circumstances, and join the glittering crew led by his little Whig.

This much decided, Mrs. Philpot made up her party, and appointed herself General-in-Chief.

My Lord Forfar was a kill-joy, and must be kept aloof. They might come on him perhaps, for his town lodging was at the Bear, over against St. Saviour's. But after his conduct over the kidnapping he must consider himself in Coventry.

Pamela might go. She loved a frolic with a spice of danger in it as much as other fine ladies. Yet, in absence of her fellow-conspirator, she would certainly be cross and vapourish. Ranulph, perhaps, might keep her in good-humour. He, of course, must go.

Mr. Falkland, the young dandy who had begun so badly at the Duchess's, was contrite now, and might go; so might Lord Belvedere, who was as dazzled and flattered by the tact of his new daughter as disgusted with the folly of the other. Since the *dénouement* of Excise he could scarce endure the sight of Mrs. Belfield, and would be thankful to anyone who, without compromising her parent, would take her off his hands. In spite of her clumsiness Mr. Medlicote was silly enough to dangle — an admirable *parti* in all ways — and she, arrant idiot, must needs snub him! It would not bear thinking of. Why couldn't the girls change places? Bab was a credit, Pamela a disgrace; cause of worry that brings wrinkles.

Colley should go with them, Bab settled, and serve as master of the ceremonies till the King arrived. Crump? He pleaded for permission with such wistful earnestness that Barbara consented.

'I'm not afraid of your presence,' she observed, with a roguish smile, '*in company*.'

And the three Miss Mostyns, with whom Bab was so very thick! Of course, they must be of the party, if only to offend Lord Forfar, should they meet that Quixote. Delightful comrades, the three Mostyns, of highest fashion—known in familiar intercourse as Crimp, Cramp, and Crumpling.

They were a lively trio, whose age might be anything 'twixt twenty and forty, so thick was their paint, so abundant their false hair. Afraid of naught else, they were so perturbed by the insipidity of existence that they were ever on the scamper from *ennui*.

Of course, it behoved such modish belles to profess dislike of anything English — just as some women dislike their husbands because they're so constantly near 'em. They affected Swiss porters, French body-servants, Indian pages; and spent so much on china, ribbons, fans, laces, washes, jessamine, gloves, and ratafia, that 'twas a marvel they were not in the spunging-house.

'Twas not possible to have run the gauntlet of the town for so many years as they had without sundry dints to reputation. But they were wont complacently to say:

'Mere flesh-wounds, if kept from the air, are not mortal, and can be prevented from appearing unsightly by a covering of silk and flowers.'

Their nights, as I need scarce state, were devoted to King Hoyle; and thus was it, many averred, that they managed to eke out an income which was mysterious and shadowy.

Such daylight as was not spent in sleep and in repairing injuries of time, was employed at Newgate or at Tyburn, ogling the dear interesting creatures in ribbons and bouquets before they leapt from the ladder into space.

The severest dint that Cramp ever received—one that called for a good deal of decoration—was dealt by the hand of the too notorious highwayman, Armstrong. She met that sweet malefactor at a ridotto, found him a pretty fellow, and having languished in orthodox fashion at his trial—kissing finger-tips towards the dock—was a little disconcerted to learn that he had been guilty of several murders.

Now, as need hardly be explained, he who points a pistol and picks a pocket is a fascinating individual, but he who fires the pistol and slays his victim is quite another animal. The whole matter turns upon blood-letting, which is odd, considering how much blood is always flowing during these years of grace.

The Mostyns were a typical trinity. They always went about together, helping each other in chorus. There was no length to which they would not go; no fatigue in pursuit of pleasure or excitement from which they would shrink; and yet they posed for valetudinarians, drooping under spleen and kindred humours, which required constant stimulants. Now Southwark Fair was just the style of entertainment to suit their jaded appetites; so they joined Bab's party with alacrity.

Mr. Falkland had been elected *nem. con.* a member of the Beaux Club in Covent Garden—nicknamed the Lady's Lapdog Club—where on a table flannel cloths were laid, for dusting upper-leathers, or specks from scabbards, or splashes from pumps of Spanish leather, which had to be kept as spot-free as a Dutch housewife's kettle.

Then there were plates of oranges and lemons for a Narcissus to polish up his nails withal. And a great box of the best perfumed powder; and, by way of garnish, an armoury of scissors, tooth-picks, tweezers, patches, essences, pomatums, points, pastes, washes, and all the implements that pride and folly can invent to turn men into monkeys.

Ah me! what a set of coxcombs! 'Tis strange that the women should have liked such creatures—beings who rarely walked, for London pavement being bad, pedestrians were condemned perforce to the wearing of thick shoes, which to fops and beaux were abominations. Of course, however, if Barbara chose to walk, her following must e'en do likewise.

Lord Belvedere was quite in his element, in a splendid suit of stamped velvet, in attendance on so brilliant a company. Sure three such butterflies as himself and Byron and Mr. Falkland never were seen out of Brazil. The youngest of the three affected languor and a weak spine; my Lord Spindleshanks tripped along like a bantam, on his drumsticks; the diplomatist, for reasons known to himself, assumed the candour of boyhood. The three Mostyns selected each a beau; and Bab, though she found herself consigned to the care of Mr. Crump, was crowned with an aureole of gaiety.

Crimp had secured Lord Belvedere, and required much skilful guidance over puddles, murmuring that there was more satisfaction in being made up to by an eminent personage than by a dozen commonplace souls; to which my lord replied that the title of beau was more precious than that of Right Honourable, for the latter may be inherited, whereas t'other must be extorted at the point of the curling-tongs from an admiring society.

'Twas a lovely day, and, dear heart! what a busy spectacle! The party had scarce crossed London Bridge ere they were besieged by a howling throng, who dragged at their skirts and strove to outshout each other.

'See "Jephthah's Rash Vow!"' bellowed one; 'an unequalled droll, trimmed with new jests and comic grins!'

'Ne'er heed him!' screeched another; 'unlike Noah's ark, only unclean beasts enter his menagerie. The life and death of Doctor Foster and all his pains! Red fire and blue! His entrails change to snakes and serpents! Wonderful!'

'Pho!' bawled a third. 'The gentry must eat first to gather strength. A dozen of oysters while five pretty wenches pipe a madrigal!'

'Pah!' roared an old beldame from her stall. 'Oysters! Cruel uncharitable meat! Why? Because they're eaten alive, and there's nothing left for the poor!'

'Oysters here!' simpered Pamela, leaning heavily on Ranulph; 'I'd as soon swallow the bung out of that beer-barrel!'

'Well said, my pretty gentlewoman!' applauded a rival opposite. 'Come hither and regale! Black pudding and seasoned sausage. I'll warrant there's no fuller's earth in *my* mustard-pan!'

'Good people,' laughed Bab, 'a modish lady would succumb under such sustenance. A daisyful of ratafia now, and a gingerbread-nut—oh!'

Ere the words were out she was seized by a dozen eager hands and borne into a booth with a blue striped tilt, wherein a band of strollers were toasting one another.

'Roast pig, you said, pretty lady?' cried a serving-man in a long apron, sharpening a huge knife. 'Here 'tis! So piping hot that it seemeth to cry, "Come, eat me!" What! No pig? Then you'll have no luck this day.'

My Lord Byron was sulky at finding himself relegated to a hag while his adored was monopolized by a rival, and, glancing at Colley, he muttered something 'twixt his teeth about the impertinent company of a nauseous scribbler, while Cramp made eyes at him. Nor was Crumpling much more successful with her partner, for indeed, as she said, Mr. Falkland took such extravagant care of the clothing of his body that his understanding went naked for it.

'Sister, your hartshorn, I implore!' simpered Cramp. 'Really these common people!'

'Lard!' cried Crimp, 'their noise is barbarous, worse than an innyard. These healthy booth-sluts are so boisterous they split one's brain!'

'Your ladyship,' laughed Bab, with a glance at Falkland, 'is too accustomed to decayed persons of quality; something so delicate that they can't speak above their breath, while the laborious effort of walking is no more than a genteel stagger!'

'Thou art a masculine creature,' sighed Crumpling plaintively. 'They set my soul on edge; do they not yours, dear Lord Belvedere? A steel-drop, my sister, or I perish!'

'Can you find anything tolerable in me?' whispered the smirking diplomatist.

'Oh indeed, my lord! a thousand taking qualities,' whispered back his fair.

'Will your ladyship do me the favour of your little finger into this booth? Say, what can you see in your humblest slave?'

'You are an ornament to your new suit, my lord. Nay, I never flatter; but 'tis plaguy hard to tell the brightest part of a diamond.'

'Strike me dumb, but you're obleeging!' returned the delighted beau. 'My suit is tolerable, I think; the buttons are three inches across, while Falkland's there, who should know better, are only of the bigness of nutmegs.'

Thus, in a genteel exchange of conceits and polished cackling, did the party advance up St. Margaret's Hill, pausing often on the way. The Diva and some of her party were speedily recognised and assailed with verbal crackers. Outside a canvas theatre a tall fellow was standing, whose arms and face showed marks of the profession of a blacksmith, but who was draped in the white robes of classic Andromache. He plumped a low curtsey, and offering a beer-pot, said in a bass voice like a trumpet:

'Mummers and grimacers, welcome! Our performance will commence anon. Come, learn, and be edified!'

'Pamela dear, he takes you for an actress,' cried mischievous Bab. 'We must watch lest you be marched to Bridewell. Mr. Crump, shall we go together and see her when she's hempbeating?'

'*We* are amateurs, not common players, and act here for our diversion,' proceeded the blacksmith, with disdain. 'Independent of authors we delineate from internal resources, with extempore screams that electrify the lieges.'

'The knave hath swallowed a dictionary,' laughed Colley Cibber. 'Give us a taste of thy powers.'

'Never heed *him*, madam,' interrupted a merry-andrew, tugging at the skirt of Crumpling. 'Favour our show. A dance of two drunken men upon a rope, comical and diverting, with other ingenious pastimes and recreations; then a trip by three wild cats of the wood, while Mr. Fawkes gets ready, the celebrated conjurer who raises a tree out of the earth with apples on it in less than a minute's time!'

Bab vowed she would visit nothing till she had walked through the fair, so, escaping from the steam and stench of the various viands in the vicinity, the party proceeded past the central pillory and cage, ignoring the wiles of a siren who, perched on the step of the machine of punishment, offered to draw a tooth, shave a gentleman, and exhibit the relics of King Solomon, all for a single groat.

Although tents and wooden edifices straggled over a large space, the principal seat of pastime was the open green which stretched behind the frowning walls of the King's Bench and Marshalsea, and was known as Snow Fields. Here was such a throng that 'twas hard to move about.

There was a central avenue, with great booths on either side, each furnished with immense pictures of wonders visible within. On the right, Mr. Pinchbeck's Theatre of the Muses, with its amazing clock that played many instruments of music with the melodious notes of many birds like real life, the tunes specially writ by Mr. Handel. His artificial world, wherein, so yelled the showman, is imitated the spangled firmament, the dawn of day, the sun diffusing his light, and his redness at even! Very marvellous! But the effect was somewhat spoilt on this occasion through the anger of the inmates of the Marshalsea, against whose wall the booth was pitched. 'Twas usual for the keepers of shows to make a collection for the debtors; but this year they made a stand, which the prisoners so resented that showers of stones were flung from within, whereby several persons were injured.

Hard by Mr. Pinchbeck's, in this the main street of the wood and canvas town, was young Mr. Fielding's theatre—a rising hack, some said he was, who had scribbled a play or two, and tried his hand at a novel. He had gathered around him a company of real comedians to go on tour among the fairs with regular plays, a puppet-motion, and a dash of pugilism, and was resolved by zeal to merit the success which he hath since earned as a novelist; for he sent forth a youth with hand-bills, stating that there was a commodious passage for the quality, with illuminated moons down the main alley at dusk, and people to conduct them to their places.

Mrs. Philpot was anxious to witness the entertainment, for there was a certain Madam Pritchard acting there, who, folks said, was clever. She could sing a song called 'Sweet, if you love me,' to meet approval; and might aspire some day to the boards of a patent house, 'twas said. But cunning Colley twitched Bab's skirt, and pointed at the bill—'The Beggar's Wedding.' Ten to one it was some garbled version of Mr. Gay's unlucky creation, and would displease Sir Robert Walpole.

Barbara's behaviour was really very bad—too shocking in a sprig of quality—though Ranulph was vastly amused at it, for he perceived that she was bent on angering Mrs. Belfield and lowering her pride; and his own treatment by that nymph was so unkind that he was not undesirous that she should be punished.

The saucy maid actually claimed acquaintance with all the strolling mummers, waving her fingers with as many nods and 'How do ye's' as a countess at a drawing-room; and when withheld from entering Mr. Fielding's, skipped over the mud across the road, and vowed she must patronize his rival.

Delicious! 'The Prison-breaker: or, The Adventures of John Shepherd. A Farce!' What more fitting than such a tale, under shadow of the King's Bench, within bowshot of the Clink, in a quarter which could boast of five jails, twenty whipping-posts and stocks, where sin and shame and sorrow have due wages?

The Mostyns were ravished. Of course they would see the delightful prison-breaker; were sorry 'twas but the counterfeit. Ten years exactly since that angel suffered, Crumpling sighed, with a languishing look at my lord. Perchance she'd known poor Jack too well, if not too wisely?

Why, it was Cibber's booth! not Colley's, of course, that magnate having retired, but Theo's, who, finding it impossible to get on with his parent, had again started for himself. 'The part of Mrs. Winifred by Madam Cibber; that of John Shepherd by Madam Charke.'

So Charlotte was here—poor wandering Charlotte! —protected by her brother, as was right. And Madam Cibber, too, in a hutch of boards! What sweet revenge to go and applaud her! In a trice Bab dropped the player and became the lady of fashion, who would condescend to patronize the mountebanks.

Colley was relieved at this moment to perceive the King coming round a corner, strutting like a little turkey-cock in front of his following of lords, and hastened to escape; while squinting Theo with an evil grin, in a tinselled robe and golden leather buskins, came forward to do the honour of his show, and place the ladies on the 'hoistings,' above low liquor and low company.

Lord Belvedere was becoming disconcerted by the warmth of Crumpling. 'Twould be laughable if she were setting a faded cap at him.

'Ged!' he muttered, 'I'm every woman's humble servant, but nothing more, at my age. An elderly man should no more bestow himself upon one woman than his sword upon a bully. Both with encouragement grew equally insolent.'

Sir Robert was enchanted with Bab's flow of spirits.

'I like to see thee gay,' he said. 'Cultivate humour, and 'twill salve all troubles. Look on mankind as a menagerie with idiosyncrasies they can't control. I mind me of a beast I saw once in a cage, that at a certain spot always turned a somersault, and then trotted gravely on. Was I angry or argumentative over that which there was no explaining? Not I. Its folly flicked my humour, and I was the better for the laugh.'

Some one was performing the interlude of the 'Footpad's Robbery,' a pantomimic dance, and played the thief so well that Sir Robert strongly suspected he must oft have done the same in earnest. He fired the pistol, stripped the victim, searched the pockets with such natural dexterity as to prove himself a master of his art; and was much applauded by the beer-swilling assembly below, who were excellent judges of the subject.

Charlotte, clad as the shock-pated housebreaker, was waiting to come on, and glancing round, perceived the distinguished party. Forgetful of the evil-eye, she advanced swiftly to the front of the platform, and pointing a finger at the Minister, cried:

'A boon, a boon! Barbara Philpot, intercede for us!'

'It shall be granted, I promise you,' returned Mrs. Philpot loftily.

'That the fairs shall not be shorn of their proportions,' Charlotte begged. 'They are meat and raiment to us poor folks, who earn our living hardly.'

'And ruin and destruction to the better sort,' grunted Sir Robert, vexed at finding himself snared.

The company rose to their feet and faced the Minister, who looked at Bab with a smile of meaning.

'Well, well!' he said; 'this is the last fair of the year. For this time be it so. Though I've caught glimpses of many a gambling-den on the way hither full of footmen and clerks, who were playing the "Prodigal Son" to a miracle!'

A shout went up which almost shook down the rafters of the crazy edifice, and caused his Majesty to marvel, who was sipping Bohea in a house hard by, built in the shape of a tea-kettle.

'Huzza for Sir Robert Walpole! Huzza! huzza!'

There was a stampede of light-fingered gentry, who were for chairing the great man all round the fair.

'Nay!' he cried, laughing; 'let us flee, or there won't be a watch or purse amongst us! Such is popularity! If only Bolingbroke were here, I could have him ducked in a twinkling.'

Barbara was so anxious to speak to Charlotte that she quite forgot her desire to gloat over her ancient enemy, and in the confusion which followed pushed a way to the back of the booth.

'Where have you been all these years?' she cried reproachfully, kissing her friend's thin face. 'Have you forgot that welcome and that dinner? Poor soul! I'm sure you've wanted it!'

But Charlotte's eyes were dancing, her wan cheek was pink with the reflected light of Hope. She was in one of her moods when all in the future seems bright and shining. Alas! 'twas with the putrid glare of the dunghill!

'I act dishonest John ten times a day,' she said, laughing, 'for the guerdon of a guinea. Brother Theophilus won't have us waste our time. When on the road we sleep where we may; when settled, in the pit, with a Dutch organ, tambourine, and Turkish jingle to lull our slumber; wake early to sweep the theatre, and throw fresh sawdust in the boxes; shake out the dresses; wind up and dust the motion-jacks; teach the dull recruits; rout the idlers from the straw, and redeem some from the watch-house. Then, the hour struck, we beat the gong and walk the stage to show our dresses; or dance with our fellows, and sing a stave, or blow the trumpet. Now and again we joke with the gathering crowd to keep them merry and lure them in; or, covering our gay habits with a coat, go down and stand opposite the booth, as if transfixed with its magnificence.'

'And you are not weary of it all?' inquired Bab.

'Are you of Drury Lane?' retorted Charlotte, who wist not of her friend's fortune.

'Indeed I know not,' Barbara murmured in abstraction.

She half envied Madam Charke her wild life, too full of stir and change for repining and regret. Would it not, indeed, be less unsatisfying to the genuine Hadji to throw sawdust in the boxes, and redeem companions from the watchhouse? There was use in such an existence. Fine-ladyism was no use on earth; that was sober truth. The Bohemian string in the girl's nature had been struck, and vibrating, produced a shudder.

'Fool! fool!' she muttered. 'Charlotte is crack-brained; and so am I, methinks! Let well alone; eschew carping discontent!' Nevertheless, when, parting from her friend, she rejoined the others to continue the day's sport, there was a shade of sadness on her face, and she could scarce find spirit even to cope with Pamela.

Finding that their swains were mawkish companions after all—so different from Tyburn fruit—the Mostyns had frisked away; but Sir Robert declared merrily that they would not be hard to find, and he was right.

Penetrating by means of a ladder, and guided by instinct, they had retired into a gaming-kennel and were hard at work, forgetting to be lackadaisical, with rattling dice, elbowing the common herd.

'I vow,' cried Crimp, when thus discovered, 'that there's nothing so engaging as to win the money of low unpolished animals!'

As the day waned the fun waxed furious, suited to the locality. Dissolute serving-men, bullies and bravos, linked arm-in-arm, swept the alleys between the booths, and catching the maids as in a net, made them pay forfeit with a kiss, while nimble fingers cut their pocket-strings. Ballad-singers, with quires of political songs under one arm, and a stool under t'other, chose out a cadging lay, but ere they had chanted a verse were pelted by some of counter-views, tripped up and floored. The concourse was so great that 'twas as merry a time for filchers as Lent for fishmongers; and there was a sprinkling of greenhorns among the fly ones whose innocence called for toll.

There was a sailor there, such a simple salt that he must needs take to buffeting a black cow that he thought to be the fiend; so doughty a mariner that he insisted in joining a sham fight against the French, whereby he smashed the apparatus. And country squires, too, with mouths as wide as mussels at the ebb, and pockets gaping! What a tempting harvest for seasoned Southwarkers while they stood or loitered, gazing at players of the back-sword, or doxies running for a smock, or the accomplished Signor Violante swinging on a rope!

Ten bargemen were advertised to 'eat ten quarts of hasty pudding, infernal hot;' he who'd done first to get ten shillings, the last a ducking. There was to be a dog dressed up in fireworks, and a cat tied to a mad bull's tail—no end of diversions. And talk of contrasts—which are as salt to an appetizing dish! The temporary town of boards in which we saunter extends in straggling streets to the end of Snow Fields, by King's Bench Garden and White Lyon Bridewell to St. George's Church—from whose summit, by-the-bye, may be obtained a splendid bird's-eye view of all that's passing. Above the tinkling of little bells that mark the progress of the festival, rises a heavy boom from the square tower. What doth it portend? Only two prisoners upon a hurdle moving to Execution Place—a brief journey of a stone's-throw only, previous to a long one. Cheek by jowl with the fair, the gibbet is always busy; the hangman the only man who may not keep holiday. His daily harvest hangs for an hour, and then is quickly plucked, to join that ripened crop in chains that is visible across the marsh.

But never heed such vermin. What is this crying and shrieking, and swaying and rushing, as a wretched female, battered and bloody, with garments rent in tatters, is pushed by myriad hands towards the ducking-stool hard by the Clink? A clyfaker? a foister? Worse. Away with the baggage! Was she not detected selling rancid tarts? and is it not stipulated in the opening proclamation at every fair, that no victual may be sold but what is wholesome for the body? No need for Marshalsea-men to interfere. Judge Lynch hath grasped his victim. While she goes souse into the muddy liquid, turn we to livelier themes.

Yonder is Mr. Figg forcing his horse against the tide, drums beating, colours flying, and a lot of big-chested fellows, with shaven pates adorned with plaster, distributing his bills. He nods in passing in glad recognition of Barbara, while Pamela perks her chin.

Just such a show is his as suits the people's fancy, and they follow in cheering crowds, for there are to be three bouts at 'threshing-flail,' some hacking and hewing by the most skilled professors, and a deft display of the art of self-defence. A space is cleared upon the green—the silence for a moment is so great that you can hear the click of the rackets in the two prison-yards—then what an appreciative roar as Figg steps out, his body marked and scored with wounds from other frays. Good lack! There's hacking and hewing in good earnest, till the place looks like the shambles, and the circling throng are convulsed with eagerness and frenzy. 'Tis splendid!

Now let's to dinner—and straightway the booths, where eatables may be procured, are full to overflowing. The inns, too, are doing a roaring trade; the galleries of the Tabard groan under the weight of the goodly company, while serving-wenches scurry to and fro with steaming dishes, and pewters of foaming ale. The Bear at the bridge-foot is the most favoured by the quality, for the view of the river is superb, alive as it is and teeming with wherries, skiffs and barges, each with a melodious band. They can look down, too, into the churchyard where citizens are picnicking upon the grave-stones; past old St. Saviour's—what a variety of stirring scenes that venerable pile hath witnessed!—into Montagu Close, a huddled heap of sordid tenements, where outcasts, ragged and hollow-eyed, are dying of famine by inches. What a zest the thought gives to the lark-pudding—to the fourth bottle of glowing burgundy! The parish dignitaries are gathered in the great reception-room on the ground-floor where marriage feasts take place, mid hubbub of jape and jest; and as his Majesty, with twenty flambeaux at his heels, takes to his gilt barge at Cockstairs, and the boat turns westward, they toast him loyally. Swashbucklers and ill-looking ruffians hang about in groups in hopes of a call to drink, assuming a modest mien that sits oddly on their truculent visages —for next door the Pie Powder Court is sitting (further from the bridge it would not dare to sit). Marshal-men are in force about the entrance, and the stocks close by and handy for such as can't claim a rescue.

With nightfall the orgy will rise to such a pitch of maniacal delirium as will be too much even for fashionable daughters of Eve. Sir Robert has had enough of it already. Mr. Falkland can scarce support the weight of his exquisite attire. The Mostyns have discovered, by furtive looks at the mirrors in their fans, that cosmetics do not improve with dust and hustling. My Lord Belvedere has no desire to spoil his new suit of rose-coloured velvet; neither has

Mr. Medlicote an ambition to be stabbed a second time. So in the gloaming the party take their boat, and fatigued, silent, listen to the plash of oars, the glittering waves of greenish light stirred in the placid waters. Barbara is dreaming of mad Charlotte and her strange way of life. Crump crouches opposite, gazing in her eyes. She has scarce vouchsafed a word to him all day! Folks must be right who vow she hath no heart. What matters it? He would even take her as she is, with all her faults and all her loveliness. A wherry passes on the silent highway, with a man and woman in it, speeding towards Gravesend. Oh that he and she were that man and woman, drifting alone together seaward! At the thought his blood tingles in his veins. To call her his very own he will dare all some day. What will he dare, and when? 'Tis worth any risk. Could anything be done with my Lord Belvedere? He will pay a visit to the diplomatist, and sound him on the earliest opportunity.

CHAPTER V.

WORRIES.

DOST thou think that the luckless Sir Robert had seen the last of Excise? No, not even yet. He was reaping the crop he had himself sown during years of contempt for the enemy.

Having recognised the necessity of changing his tactics, the tumult which arose in consequence was as great as though he were inaugurating some fresh outrage. A room may not be swept without the raising of dust. Though he was compelled to bow his head, contrary to conviction, before public opinion, he was not the man to be dictated to by subordinates in office, or endure traitors in his camp.

Cobham, Burlington, Marchmont, Stair, received a rough *congé*. The Dukes of Bolton and Montrose were ousted from their appointments and military commands. His Grace of Bolton's impudent conduct almost succeeded in ruffling Sir Robert's calm. Had he not drawn £5,000 a year for ever so long from the secret-service account, which his Duchess, erst actress Polly, frivolled away in pins; and, when came the tug of war, had he not babbled of a conscience and turned against his leader? Conscience, quotha! He might have found it earlier.

'Twas laughable to consider the Dawley high-road —'twas crowded by discomfited sinecurists on their way openly to join the enemy. The air of the Dawley dining-parlour was thick with anathemas, as they confided Bluestring to the care of Lucifer in bumpers of St. John's claret.

Barbara, to the growing annoyance of Mrs. Belfield, was quite a heroine at court. The story of that supper-party had reached the Queen's ears, though she pretended ignorance, and Bab was accordingly much considered.

Medlicote was waxing weary of Pamela's cruelty. She really was almost too pronounced in her rudeness, even for a lord's daughter. Hence he and Sir Robert and Bab found themselves sitting frequently in a solemn conclave, in which Mrs. Belfield had no part.

In the first gush of quick resentment the Queen had been for banishing Pamela; but Sir Robert good-naturedly interceded. He made the most of the scene at St. Stephen's, where he vowed he had been nearly murdered; and whispered mysteriously of the vessel at Gravesend and of Barbadoes; but since a man can gain no credit by fighting with a woman, Mrs. Pamela must be spared. Moreover she was the child of Belvedere, who in his way had been useful, and might be again. That he had naught to do with the kidnapping, Sir Robert felt assured. As for the vixen and her Jacobite, 'twas enough to know them for enemies.

Both Bab and Ranulph were against the too vigorous and too tardy use of the besom. The late high-handed measures served to swell and re-invigorate the hostility of Opposition; and, as Bab pointed out, there would be a general election ere many months were gone, before which it behoved the Whigs to conciliate the masses, who had been so stirred by Excise. The enemy was aware of this, and, too eager, made a false step. Pulteney rose in the House, and, pointing at Walpole, said:

'I am persuaded he still entertains the same opinion of the Excise, and only awaits a proper opportunity to renew it.'

Sir Robert at once took advantage of the blunder. A chance of gracefully making public recantation was just what he wanted, so, rising at once, he declared hotly that, being the public's faithful servant, he was not so mad as ever again to engage in anything that at all looked like an Excise. A frank statement, most satisfying to the people.

Bolton and Cobham feebly attempted to rouse sympathy on their behalf, in that they had lost bread and cheese for conscience' sake. What hath a man's behaviour in Parliament, bleated Bolton, to do with the performance of duty in a military capacity? But he only got laughed at for his pains, for 'twas notorious that Bolton had nothing about him of the soldier except the uniform, and much preferred hazard at the coffee-house to prancing on the field of glory.

Was there, indeed, no means of undermining this too sturdy Bluestring? Opposition were as unfortunate in the Lords as in the Commons; invertebrate on both arenas. Marlborough brought up the subject, and was brilliantly supported by Chesterfield; but to no purpose. Fair means would not do. Bluestring was stronger than ever, and growing day by day in popular esteem. The Dawley moles must take to earth again, and worm with secret burrowing.

Though subjected by events to hot and cold fits, Mrs. Belfield, having made up her mind, still resolved to adhere to the doubtful fortunes of Lord Forfar. The scheme had been in perfect train, and but for that diabolical *fine-mouche*, would have resulted in triumph. She detested Walpole now for Barbara's sake as well as for her own, and the wish being father to the thought, felt convinced that, his personal influence removed, the Brunswicks would collapse like a pricked bladder.

What she saw daily at court helped her conviction,

for indeed the King grew crosser and more fidgety day by day; the Queen more tired and harassed; while as for my Lady Suffolk, she did nothing but groan and cry. Fred was becoming a grievous thorn in the regal pillow. Thinking much of his own parts, he was a mere shuttlecock of party, tossed hither and thither, respected by none; as a thorn to his parents only could he be deemed a success.

When George and Frederick met they glared and did not speak, and the ruffling of respective Bobadils was exaggerated accordingly, till the conduct in the street of the two sides resembled that of Orsinis and Colonnas.

Fred had a weaker understanding, and, if possible, a more obstinate temper than his papa, and was, moreover, false and deceitful, which his papa was not. Not but what he had a good deal to bear, for his father abhorred him, his mother despised him, his sisters disliked and betrayed him, his servants and adherents made a fool of him.

To gratify alike his loathing and his avarice, George held his purse-strings tight. Money was dribbled out capriciously, the result of which was that the Prince of Wales's treasury was always empty, and his creditors importunate. He coquetted clandestinely with Opposition, hoping to turn their present discomfiture to future use, they employing his distress to discredit his family. Indeed, the conduct of father and son was a by-word of what was disreputable; and Pamela was justified in supposing that if the prop were withdrawn, so contemptibly weak an edifice must topple.

'Twas a case of mutual propping. If one could be deprived of t'other, both must fall together. When she related to willing ears the family episodes at St. James's, the eyes of Gervas brightened. The prop should be withdrawn. Before retiring underground again with the moles, he would go forth on a forlorn-hope, and break a last lance with Bluestring. If his own were shivered, why, other means must be resorted to. So he appeared one day at Dawley, and seeking out Bolingbroke and Chesterfield, who were daintily examining the hay through quizzing-glasses, announced his resolution.

My Lord Chesterfield snuffled (he suffered woundily from hay-fever—odious complaint, unknown in more favoured town), and disapproved. Where he, Chesterfield, had failed, 'twas impudent in this plodding Jacobite to suppose he might succeed. Not so Bolingbroke. There is a Providence, he thought, that watches over enthusiasts as well as drunkards. This absurd fellow had somewhat the bearing of a true ascetic knight, sallying forth after the Grail. Had he not already won his spurs in Parliament, and gained respect there? Let him go and try. He, the banished Bolingbroke, would arm the champion; rivet his greaves of steel. Alack! the worldling had better have left the knight to arm himself; but St.

John could never permit a chance to escape of hurling his venom at Walpole. 'Twas he who professed no principles, who had intrigued with and betrayed every party, who was the most virulent denouncer of the head and front of corruption.

Like a David sallying forth against Goliath, Gervas was to have his way and smite the giant. The attack was led off by Pulteney, skilled skirmisher. Then up rose Lord Forfar in his place, and the House was hushed; for he was cold, dignified, and eloquent. He had never spoken better; and Bolingbroke had never been more careful in priming a disciple. But there was an absence of that convinced enthusiasm on which the wily farmer had counted.

'Twas evident that Gervas was glowing with reflected malignity as, his dark eyes fixed steadily on the Chief Minister, he drew his portrait. He sketched a man abandoned by all vestiges of virtue or honour; of mean fortune and no family, raised by whimsical events to the post of commander-in-chief—one who cared for nothing but himself; who, so that he prospered, heeded not the nation's interest neglected, her credit lost, her trade insulted, her merchants plundered; who became thus possessed of much ill-gotten wealth, presiding over a puppet Parliament —the seats purchased, the votes bought at the expense of the public treasury. Then he filled in the outline. Secure of his packed jury, ready to acquit him in all adventures, this bloodsucker tarantula arrived, in natural course, at so insolent a degree of arrogance as to domineer over men of sense and figure, who were weak enough to be scrupulous; and, having no virtue of his own, ridiculed it in others, striving to corrupt and strangle it. Supposing this person to exist—the speaker hoped so dire a monster never did or could—his audience were further to suppose a foreign Prince, ignorant and unacquainted with the interests and inclinations of his people. Supposing such a Prince solely advised by such a Minister, supported by such a Parliament, what hope was there for the devoted nation? None, but in speedy repentance. By wriggling, intriguing, bargaining himself into a position to which he was not called by general suffrage, this wretch had risen to power. The Prince might yet be enlightened: the Minister was beyond redemption; there was no fit fate for such a scourge but annihilation, thorough and complete!

Members twittered like birds before a thunderstorm. Smiling, Walpole rose, and ignoring the dark-eyed speaker, proceeded to sketch another portrait, that of the well-known adversary of whom the enthusiast was merely a mouthpiece.

'Dear me,' he said jocosely, with dumpy hands plunged into waistcoat-pockets, while his fat cheeks shook. 'Wicked Ministers, domineering Ministers, insolent Ministers! Sure, they must flourish in some far-off land visited by Gulliver! May I go also on my travels? I see a most unfortunate country ruled by another Minister—a fine gentleman, who, supposing himself to be the only sane man in a community of lunatics, dubs all the others Blunderer. This person suffers from a disappointed and malicious heart, and, gagged himself, shoots forth black poison through others' mouths! Permitted by too great mercy to live in a land wherein he is unfit to dwell, he uses every art, weighted as he is by the contempt of all mankind, to sap the fountain from whence that mercy flowed. He hath been in many lands, and everywhere made it his trade to betray the secrets of every court where he had been before. An unfortunate country in truth, with such a monster! Worse than my Lord Forfar's picture is mine, for can there be imagined a greater disgrace to human nature than such a scoundrel?'

When he sat down there was a general murmur of congratulation; and Ranulph, in his excitement, rushed to his friend and clasped him warmly by the hand; for though invective may be considered by some an ornament of debate, it was felt by all who were not madly blinded that Lord Forfar's strictures were unjust and coarse. 'Twas so unlike himself to have thus spoken, that men turned on him a pitying look, which brought the blood welling to his brow.

'Wriggling and intriguing,' forsooth! It was just like St. John. Walpole was the acknowledged and trusted leader of the great Whig party, who, though he might trip, as all fallible men are prone to do, put faith in his growing administrative eloquence, financial finesse, tact in the management of men. There could be no denying that, his hand on the helm, the country was at peace with its neighbours, and its commerce on the increase. Gervas was blamed, therefore, on all sides for the unwarrantable attack; and people said openly that ere next he primed his pupil, Bolingbroke should look at home. 'Twas a pity so good a man as Forfar should be so much under St. John's influence. A crowded chamber warmly cheered Walpole's retort, and some who had been chill rallied round him in the hour of insult.

Pulteney, perceiving the egregious mistake that had been made, ground his teeth and bit his nails in silence. Gervas felt ashamed; for he saw now that he had been snared by his master into direct untruth —untruth that was patent and discernible. A little untruth that was not discernible, though to be deprecated, was admissible, for everything must be suffered for 'the Cause;' and yet, when he realized how strongly the tide of opinion was against him, there entered the mind of the Jacobite a glimmer that perhaps he was himself deceived, pursuing a corpse-light into a bog.

His lance had shivered in his grasp, and he felt the tingling of the shock up to the elbow. In the ordeal by battle, wherein Heaven sides with the right, he had been worsted. The forlorn-hope was a failure. The Cause was a right and holy one—the forementioned glimmer, that it might possibly be otherwise, sent a shudder of horror to the roots of his hair. Oh yes! it was a right and holy one—it must be, or his whole life and career were a mistake; and any weapons were to be used to achieve its triumph. But he was unusually perturbed in mind, and had lost much of his usual serenity when, riding to Bushey, he passed through the gates of Lord Belvedere's villa to report progress to Mrs. Belfield.

The forlorn-hope had been the last struggle of the session, and wearied legislators had left town lodgings. The King and Queen were at Hampton Court; the Duchess at Richmond; everybody else in their cots about the river.

Who so wroth as Pamela as she listened to Gervas, who, bridle over arm, walked slowly up and down the grass plot and told his tale? That odious woman was upstairs at a window, and, if the news had reached her yet, must be laughing in her sleeve at them. Gervas was gloomy and mysterious. What was passing in his mind? Was he endeavouring to stifle a doubt in the successful issue of the Cause? That would be too terrible! For had she not gone too far for retreat? That tale about the kidnapping, and the part she was supposed to have taken in it, had been spread abroad by Bab. At least Pam suspected it shrewdly, for modish friends were cold, and giggled behind their fans, though they said naught. Was it too late for retreat? Was it advisable to retreat if possible? Angels, they say, prefer those who have fallen and got up again, to those who have never stumbled. It would not do to retreat, and, finding herself wrong after all, to fall between two stools.

Why would this man enwrap himself in mystery? How she longed to box his ears! Somehow since she had become his spy, and the two had conspired deliciously in corners, she had grown less afraid of the Jacobite, although, for obvious reasons, she still showed her prettiest side to him. What was the next move to be? The Dawley junta were discredited. If the cause was not to rely on something less unstable than their help, 'twould be better to give it up. But at the time of the kidnapping he had unfolded all sorts of plans—or rather had hinted of the existence of such—which would alone have justified so startlingly desperate an expedient as bottling and corking a Minister.

As they walked up and down and laid their heads together, Bab looked from the window, cheek on hand; and was in no mood for laughing, whether in her sleeve or out of it. The sprig of quality was drooping in uncongenial soil. That was what ailed the maid.

'Twas vain to take herself to task about it, to endeavour by force of will to subdue unruly nature.

Argue as she might, the feeling of discontent was growing apace. 'Must I always hanker for that I may not have?' she kept repeating in vain. To seek forbidden fruit is a need in woman's life. The garden of Eden would be a humdrum bore to more ladies than our first mother, who without the serpent's tempting would some day have tasted the apple. What had been the use of praying for a father, and building up hopes on the possibility of the prayer being answered? It was coming home to her, as it does in time to most of us, that in nine cases out of ten 'tis presumptuous impertinence in the human beetle to dare to crave at all. All-seeing Providence knows best, and 'tis better to accept things as they are given. The father whom it would have been so pleasant to obey, when he became a reality turned out to be—a snuffbox! 'He would not give his powder-puff to save my soul,' his daughter thought. A clever diplomatist he might be; but his sterling qualities were so rolled up and wrapped, that 'twas impossible for the purposes of weekaday existence to pierce the swaddling.

Crazy Charlotte's idle seed was swelling. Did she not regret Drury Lane? The question put thus frankly demanded a reply. There existence had a meaning; and how much more lively was the Lock of Hair, with the tittle-tattle of the beaux in curl-papers, than this damp villa. We never know when we're well off, she reflected. Time was when amid daily and hourly incense she had complained that no one could love the player save from the temporary point of view. Well, she was no longer a player, but a lady of fashion received at court; and how much was she thereby benefited? Nobody loved her now, any more than then. Nothing could be much more unpleasant than the *ménage à trois* of which she had formed a part. Her father liked her because she was admired. Should she take small-pox in a virulent form, how gladly would he be quit of her!

Pamela's affection was of the spitfire kind which may be observed at night upon the tiles. And what did she get in exchange for what she had relinquished? Nothing but vexation of spirit and weariness of soul. True, she had been privileged to save her hero in a ticklish strait, but she could not expect to be always saving Walpole; nay, even if that were possible, like all else 'twould grow monotonous. None, that she was aware, was the better for her existence. That wretched Pamela pacing up and down below was a disagreeable sight to look upon. As Bab lugubriously meditated, she grew hot and angry; for 'twas provoking to perceive how the Jacobite was being hoodwinked. Now, had she, Bab, been gifted with the affections of such a man as that, how her nature would have ripened and improved; what lovely leaves of good would have been unfolded! But he was too busy with his Cause for lovemaking. Concerning what could he be always chattering to that malapert? Were they plotting another snare under her nose? Foolish Pamela! Did she think that the rosy god would intervene for her behoof in the midst of her conspiracies? That was not likely, thank goodness! Why should she be thankful? What was Gervas to her? Flushed and startled, angry with herself, Bab rose and quitted the window. There was a sound of hoofs upon the gravel. Walpole and his secretary were riding up the drive, perceiving whom, Pamela and her conspirator dived into a side walk and disappeared among the bushes.

While Sir Robert chatted with Barbara, Mr. Crump sought out Lord Belvedere. Though Walpole had turned Bolingbroke's last weapon against himself, he was far from easy in his mind. Complications were arising of which the enemy would take every advantage. The Minister had no doubt but that he would gain the best of the conflict; yet it would be a difficult battle, and the harassed warrior longed for a brief respite wherein to close the eyes of vigilance and indulge in forty winks.

Riding to Hampton Court, he had resolved to stop at Bushey, and converse with his little Whig. Her suggestions were always sensible; and, at any rate, 'twould be a comfort to unburthen himself. Oftentimes in explaining a matter to some one else it becomes the clearer to ourselves; and the new looming trouble that now peeped over the horizon threatened to be tangled and intricate. Trouble was a hydra—the Excise-head having been chopped off, there was yet more work to do; for another was coming into existence to gnash at him.

The title of which Sir Robert was most proud was that of 'Minister of Peace.' He had always striven to keep England out of foreign squabbles whilst maintaining her dignity intact, and had so far been successful. But now a circumstance had occurred which threatened a European war, and the Dawley junta would certainly leave no effort untried to drag their enemy into it.

Augustus, King of Poland, was just dead; and the crown being elective, two candidates presented themselves. One was Stanislaus, protected by the King of France; the other, son of the deceased, was befriended by the Austrian Emperor, and the Czarina of all the Russias. The nucleus, this, of a very pretty quarrel, such as should find occupation for all the armies of Europe. England, from her isolated position, might well hope to keep out of the *mêlée*. But unhappily his Majesty was bellicose; for though Britain was cut off by the silver streak, beloved Hanover was in the midst of the scrimmage, and unless protected might be a sufferer.

The point concerning which the Minister discoursed was whether his influence and that of the Queen, who blindly followed him, were sufficient to work upon the King when Herrenhausen was in question. Englishmen were always jealous of the King's Hanoverian proclivities, and 'twould be a grievous missile in the hands of the foe at the general election if they could point to British armies careering over Europe for the good of the petty principality.

Bolingbroke and his party were at this moment plunged into the direst depths of despair; but so soon as they should perceive what was in the wind, they would be up again, forging new arms to plunge into the hated midriff.

Barbara, with her hands clasped behind her back, considered.

'My advice,' she said presently, 'is to push your recent tactics of severity yet a step further. I deprecated the movement at the time, but you were right. You have found it needful to punish false friends by thrusting them forth into the cold. My Lord Bolingbroke wanted t'other day to ship your worship across seas. Why not imitate so worthy an example, and drive him across the water?'

'What! Ship him to the Indies?' laughed Walpole.

'No. Exile him. Dawley is too near London.'

'On what plea? 'Twas a pity he was ever permitted to come home; but, being here, he cannot well be exiled for scurrilous libels in a paper. The *Craftsman* always stops just short of actual treason.'

'So long as he is in England you will have no rest,' rejoined Bab. 'What if there was a Jacobite plot afoot? As things are, 'twould be odd if he were not the head of it.'

'No such luck,' replied Walpole, sighing. 'They are all in my pay, so I know what passes. They are distressingly somnolent. The Chevalier himself is always drunk; his following replete and sleek, and overfed—with my money.'

'You eagles are so busy scanning the horizon,' smiled Barbara, 'that what is passing under your nasal appendage escapes your vision. Which of the paid spies warned you of your peril t'other day?'

Sir Robert still appearing incredulous, Bab explained that Lord Forfar and Mrs. Belfield were hatching something; she was sure of it. Otherwise, what could they have to talk about so often, and so secretly? At this very minute they were hard at work somewhere in the grounds; their behaviour exactly what it had been previous to the kidnapping.

'Oh, you women!' cried Sir Robert, with a roar of laughter. 'You think no one hath charms but your individual selves. Sure, Mrs. Belfield sees not an ugly phiz in her own glass, and hath persuaded the guileless Scotchman! They are talking of their wedding, depend upon it.'

Meanwhile, Mr. Crump had found my Lord

Belvedere as uneasy and preoccupied as everyone else. His valet had laid out a fresh consignment from France with such artful labour, that 'twould have been a pity to touch lest the harmony of garments should be broken. Ten wigs of a row appealed for admiration on their blocks. A 'story,' a 'bob,' a 'tie,' a 'queue,' a 'George,' a brand-new full periwig, *chef-d'œuvre* of Lauder — stood temptingly in vain.

My lord was morose, and, forgetful of enamel, crumpled his visage into puckers. Was it not horrible, having steered a bark cleverly for no matter how many decades, to find himself capsized into the water by the female foolishness of his own flesh?

The diplomatist was in a quandary, utterly unable to see his way. He had kept out of the kidnapping with infinite tact; had so arranged his attitude as— in neither of two contingencies—to be the loser.

Bab had on a memorable occasion covered herself with glory, and he had expressed his feelings by kissing her extremest finger-tips.

Pamela had made a fool of herself; but, when rated, instead of crying *peccavi*, had tilted her nose, and said something impertinent about mumbling dotards.

'Twas not conceivable that she, acidulated damsel, should show such *aplomb*, such self-sacrificing *sang-froid*, unless there was something behind. What could there be behind? Now that he had had time to study his darling child, 'twas evident that she did nothing without a reason, and that she was not one to come to shipwreck on the rock of sentiment.

The boldness of the kidnapping plot was worthy of commendation. 'Twas the first link of a chain the rest of which was for the time concealed.

Lord Belvedere argued, as Pamela herself had argued, that so audacious a thing would not be attempted unless other audacities were ready wherewith to follow up the advantage. What could they be? After the failure of the plot, Pamela had retained so calm a front as to deceive even her astute parent, who gave her credit for knowing more than she really did.

Given that there was more behind, Sir Robert's triumph was perhaps temporary? Like his daughter, he thought of the two stools; but in his case the agony was more acute, for the other daughter was, in her way, equally sanguine and serene; and 'twas vastly disagreeable to be so uncertain as to which of his children he should cling to, which disown.

Clearly Pamela must be behind the scenes and know what was going forward, or she never could keep up that high-bred air of nonchalance. Besides, something had happened of a strictly private nature, which had confirmed this view. Lord Forfar had called on him, and in the coolest fashion had asked whether at a future period he might claim his daughter's hand.

'Odsheartikins!' her parent had replied, after the first surprise, 'you may marry her for me! She deems herself wiser than her father, and hath a natural aversion to a husband of his choosing; having learnt enough of the world to be thoroughly disobedient on occasion.'

Knowing her as now he did, Pamela would never have authorized a poor Scotch lord to ask such a question unless she was certain of the future. But then it had suddenly transpired that he had not been authorized, that before putting the question to the lady his old-world punctilio had deemed it needful to obtain the father's consent.

This put Lord Belvedere in a mighty passion. A consent had been drawn from him under false pretences. And yet what could he mean by a 'future time,' except the not too far distant moment when the King over the water would have his own again? And then had come that fiasco in the House. The man was a visionary—unpractical, dreamy. Lord Belvedere had also been looking out of window, quite as much displeased as Barbara; and had then and there resolved to speak plainly to the Scotchman. It would not do for himself and his daughter to be compromised by dreamy whimsies. Since he had chosen to put himself in the position of a suitor, the Jacobite must lay his cards on the table.

What did he propose? The dowry which could be scraped together for Mrs. Belfield would not keep a husband and a crop of children. What were my lord's prospects? That he had wasted his patrimony was notorious.

The sight of Walpole and Crump riding up the drive at this juncture had exasperated Lord Belvedere to the pitch of forgetting his enamel, and turning pettishly from the French consignment.

Here was Walpole—triumphant, at all events, now. What would he think upon seeing the man who, after trying to kidnap, had grossly insulted him, making himself at home on the lawn of one whom he called friend? Despite his ingenuity he would be looked on as one of the false ones, and be cast into outer darkness along with Cobham, Bolton, Grafton—he who had been angling so ingeniously to get fresh employment abroad, or a snug post at home.

It was a relief when the two absurd delinquents had the grace to plunge into the bushes. Verily, Bab was the really clever one. All things considered, it would be best to stick to her, and make much of the powers that were.

He was glad to see Mr. Crump, and have a good talk over affairs; for he could cope with Crump, whereas he always had a dim suspicion that Walpole's *bonhomie* concealed distrust.

The King had been complimentary at the first

Drawing-room he had attended on his return, so had Sir Robert. But there had as yet been no mention of fresh employment; and 'twas now some months since he had left the Hague. Being a man of the world, he had long learnt the lesson that the servants of great men are greater men; that to get well within the doors of the powerful you must cringe to the porter, pay your devoirs to the gentleman, and must smile for half an hour on the footman ere you can hope for a nod from the master.

Thus was it that his own household, as representative of majesty abroad, had been managed; and, so that he could gain an object in view, he had no objection himself to truckle. So he embraced Mr. Crump with a salute on both cheeks, and gave his attention to that worthy.

Honest Jack explained the position of affairs abroad lucidly; and my lord, who at first nursed a leg, and reflected with one eye closed that the calves of his stockings might be padded with advantage the thickness of a crown-piece less, was soon entirely absorbed in the more serious subject.

Here was a new light thrown, and a vivid one! Might its radiance assist the wight who groped in the dusky labyrinths of State?

When Gervas made his fiasco in the House, he knew nothing of this Polish difficulty—ergo, St. John knew naught of it, or he would have used it in preparing the attack. Why, what a caldron was on the fire! France, of course, would go all lengths to support the father of France's queen, Stanislaus. On the other hand, Austria would invade Silesia; Russia would pour an army over Lithuania. What of Holland, Hanover, the Rhine?

The diplomatist came to the front, the beau fell into the background; and Crump looked upon Lord Belvedere as he was, unswaddled by lace and velvet. He saw a wrinkled old man in a handsome brocade dressing-gown and nightcap wig, whose little eyes were as bright as a ferret's, while his thin lips were wreathed in caustic smiles. Could he, Crump, get round this astute old schemer? Yes; by playing on his selfishness. Crump was no fool, neither, despite his lack of book-learning, save in his unsuccessful love adventure.

Cardinal Fleury, Chief Minister of France, whilst pretending as deep-seated a fondness for peace as Walpole, could not but be carried by the stream.

'Don't trust him!' rapped out the diplomatist. 'Double-faced and slippery. What of the King? There lies the point.'

'No doubt,' acquiesced Honest Jack, 'all Germans have a natural aversion to the French. As Hanoverian Elector he will lean to his German chief, the Emperor, and take sides against Stanislaus. And yet a war about a King of Poland, at a time when the elections are coming on, would be mighty hazardous for us. Hence, there will be no war—in spite of the efforts of Opposition, to whom no fuel could be so effectual to fan the flame of discontent—until the elections are well over. England will allow the dogs to fight over the bone for a time, and then come forward as arbitrator. Meanwhile each power, hoping to win the English King to friendship, will allow his subjects to exercise their commerce freely. After receiving favours on all hands, while others receive blows, the British authorities will be able, in opulence and prosperity, to give favour to those who've brought themselves to poverty and distress. This is Sir Robert's plan, which he unfolded to me as we rode hitherward.'

'Ingenious,' thought the diplomatist appreciatively. ' Can I doubt which is the stronger?'

'The Jacobites have made so many false steps of late,' continued Crump, 'that no one trusts them. The Court of Vienna has already sent to us to ask for succour; also to the United Provinces. No one should know better than your lordship what will be the answer from the States-General. London and the Hague must act in concert; and to that end a sagacious envoy must forthwith and secretly go thither. Who better fitted than Lord Belvedere to revisit his old campaigning ground; and, having helped to work out a particularly difficult problem, receive a grateful country's thanks?'

My lord blinked with ferret-eyes upon the speaker.

' Opposition, though foiled for a moment, is strong,'

he observed doubtfully. 'Am I to understand that this visit of yours is an ambassage?'

Crump returned his glance and smiled.

'The swell of the sea continues after the storm is over,' he remarked. 'I have much credit with Sir Robert, or could not speak so plainly. But we do nothing for nothing in this world.'

So! 'Twas to be a compact between my lord and the secretary, who was set to sound him. No wonder that his loyalty should be thought doubtful, after Pamela's unwisdom. On the report of the secretary much might depend.

'An appointment to so delicate a mission,' said the diplomatist, 'is worth much. Past services are often dumb. How shall I repay this one?'

'By the gift of your daughter,' replied Crump, so quietly as to take my lord's breath away.

'What!' he gasped. 'To whom?'

'To me.'

Lord Belvedere recovered himself, and said, with an arch leer:

'Ged! You're a liquorish dog, stap my vitals, and would snap high! There are too many who gape for favours without chance of a return; and yet methinks this one would be dearly paid. Miss Belfield——'

'May go hang herself for me!' roughly retorted Crump, who chafed under the old beau's sneer. 'Give me Barbara, and I am your devoted servant.'

My lord was genuinely staggered. Mr. Crump's position was, to outward seeming, a good one, and improving daily. This very conversation showed the consideration in which he stood with Sir Robert. That one so far-seeing and adroit as Walpole would eventually get the better both of the dreamers and the malicious was now so patent to his lordship that he wondered how he ever could have doubted it. 'Twas as though scales had fallen from his eyes. To marry the Honourable Pamela to such a man as Crump was out of the question—indeed, the damsel herself would have words to say on that subject—but he would do well enough for Bab, who, if charming, suffered under a disadvantage. The match would be most fitting, for was not she the ally of the Minister, while her proposed husband was his trusted agent?

Lord Belvedere cheerfully gave his consent, and felt a weight taken off his mind. Heads or tails? Heads it was—Sir Robert's. A private and convenient moment must be chosen to trounce the benighted Belfield and send the Scotchman packing.

Sir Robert and his secretary mounted and rode onward to Hampton Court; and Gervas, having waited till they were well away, got on his horse and trotted Dawleywards.

Pamela, when she emerged from the bushes, was radiant. Gervas, skilfully played, had been landed, and being brought to book by the calculating fair before she would whisper 'yes,' had, under seal of strictest secrecy, made a clean breast of hopes and plans and aspirations. She was right. Of course, all along she had been right. 'Twas so like the fatuity of vain dotards to drone and cry out, ' Beware !' The plot, as in its ramifications she saw it clearly now, was a splendid one, and bound to be successful if slowly and cautiously carried out. Gervas was in constant intercourse with James III.—had money-bonds of his in his pocket, which she had seen and fingered. Everything was going as smoothly as possible, and 'twas for the best that Walpole and his myrmidons should be lulled into a seeming security by an evanescent triumph, while the ground was being delved from under their feet.

Gervas, with his vampire smile, had said that for her sake he would be worldly. What a puss it was to care for such things ! A dukedom, and pelf to gild the coronet? Of course, he could not and would not make stipulations on the subject, but solemnly promised to work on James's gratitude while it was warm. When comfortably seated on the throne, he would no doubt say to those who had placed him there, 'What do you wish? Substantial service deserves reward.'

'Twas the old story. In putting forth his eloquence to persuade her that all was well, he had persuaded himself. The vague qualms of which he had been fitfully conscious were felt no more. He was to strain each nerve to tightest tension; she was to do the like, and in course of time the ripened plot would burst upon the town, and among other wonders the new Duke and Duchess would appear and amaze the lieges. 'Twas a pity, he reflected as he rode along, that she should lay so much stress upon money and coronet; 'twas earthy, and rather spoiled the picture of ethereal bliss that he was contemplating. And then he laughed softly and tenderly. Like all girls, she loved gewgaws; was unusually careful and methodical; would make the best of spouses for one who confessed himself wanting in the wisdom of the children of Mammon. He must not blame her. Had he not explained to himself long ago that, embittered by circumstance, she would, under the fostering warmth of his loving care, shake off the brown-nipped leaves that marred the plant?

Lord Forfar was satisfied as he rode Dawleywards; and so was Pamela as, emerging from the secluded walk, she was stealing to her chamber to indulge in golden day-dreams of ambition and success. Oh fall of fairy palace! Oh crumbling of heaven-reaching towers made of cloud! Lord Belvedere summoned her into his sanctum among the wigs and fop-covers, and, with scant respect for her radiant visage, his speech was brief and unvarnished. The harsh shrill tones of the Honourable Pamela soon rose above his sharp ones, and there was such a clatter that the listening valet fled appalled. Was the fair disconsolate? did she sigh, and moan, and plead, and melt in harrowing protestations? Not a bit of it. With arms akimbo, and tongue which in its blunt knowledge of what it should not know even astonished her papa, she returned him—pit-a-pat—a Roland for his Oliver; and then with throat and lips convulsed, and brow as black as night, she whisked like a fury from his presence. Did she seek her room like a wounded animal stealing to the covert? No. She dashed into the chamber of her sister, who, expecting no evil, was sipping Chinese drink, her mind bent on foreign war and home politics. Hoighty-toighty! The fight was come at last which both combatants had long foreseen. They had walked warily round each other ever since that first night when Bab was taken home; had executed feints and sly manœuvres; had saluted, and stamped, and lunged, and recovered, and stood with rapier poised and courteous simpers. But here was the tug of war, and Bab, quietly depositing her cup, was charmed.

'And so, you mumping beggarly whining mountebank!' cried Pamela, out of breath, but sparkling with ire, 'what have we done that, falling like a shadow of ill upon a peaceful house, you should be an abiding curse? My father and I would have jogged on well enough, but for your baleful presence.

I have borne more—much more—than a woman of rank and spirit should. Who are you? A cozening forgery, born of some hedge-drab, dropped from Lord knows where, to sicken us with pinchbeck graces!'

'Your servant!' retorted Bab, with a cold scorn that set Pamela's blood tingling. 'I will study polite manners from your ladyship.'

'Your roystering Mostyns and braggart train of Mohock debauchees,' pursued Mrs. Belfield, 'have turned your silly head! You raddled image! what have we done that you should set us by the ears?'

'What is my crime?' inquired Bab, with a sweet smile; for 'twas vastly pleasant to see how ugly her sister looked when torn with rage. 'Is it my fault that I should have read you from the first as you really are? A living lie—a cold scheming coquette in every wicked limb?'

'You mushroom skipjack!' jeered Mrs. Belfield.

'Faugh! What a slimy snake!' retorted her sister.

'I'll—I'll—wash thy face with thy tea!' hissed quivering Pamela.

'You who were not born under a hedge,' scoffed naughty Bab, 'where, pray, did you learn depravity? The quality care not what's said of 'em, since there's no need for shame under a mask of brass.'

'Puffed by a dotard's whim, you have forgot your

station. Though bastards are only fit for concubines, my father in his goodness hath provided you a spouse. Leave mine alone, then.'

'Your spouse—and mine?' cried Bab, astounded.

'You've set my father, mischievous trull, to rob me of my lord; but 'twill be vain.'

'Your lord—I!' gasped Mrs. Philpot.

'Dost think I'm blind?' sneered Mrs. Belfield; 'I've watched and laughed to see you worm for him; barefaced effrontery! That he of all men should swallow a bend sinister!'

Bab being apparently struck dumb, Pamela pursued her advantage as, with nervous laughter, she picked her fan to shreds.

'I protest 'tis diverting. Lord Forfar of all men! You were a madwoman to dream that one so proud would stain his scutcheon! Patience, poor hussy, for I love him not. Anon I'll freely hand him over to your ladyship if you aspire to the post of mistress.'

The colour was ebbing slowly from the face of her antagonist, as with lips apart she clasped her hands over her bosom, so Pamela pushed briskly forward into the country of the foe.

'The spider,' she tittered, 'would gobble all the flies! Why not be bachelor's wife to Medlicote, if he will have you? Matrimony and Crump will be dull to one so rakish.'

'Crump!' ejaculated the other, turning from white to red.

'No need for shuffling! My father hath told me that you are promised to the uncouth fellow.'

'Gervas!' gasped Bab. 'Lord Forfar hath proposed—to you——'

'And is accepted. Gervas indeed! Insolent wench! He hath asked me to be his, and shall be, despite your malice. He shall know that you've sighed for him in vain, and then what diversion for him and me! But Lard! we shall be a modish couple, and I not jealous, for I despise him. To hob and nob with one so fatuous would make one die of yawning!'

'Is it indeed so?' Bab replied slowly. 'Ill-starred, unhappy man—worthy of a kinder fate!'

There was a profound contempt and mournful conviction of certain misfortune as result of a match with Pamela in Mrs. Philpot's tones, more hard to bear than bandied epithets.

Stung to the quick, Mrs. Belfield murmured, 'You impudent slut!' and banged out of the chamber.

With which lay the victory? The Honourable Pamela had suddenly retreated from the field; but Mrs. Philpot was desperately buffeted.

Left alone, she sat her down to think; but 'twas long ere whirling thoughts would take coherent shape.

It was not mere plotting then, as she had supposed. Gervas, the true and upright, had asked this wicked woman to tie herself to him—for life! He loved her, then? How could he?

'Oh, silly, silly men!' she murmured, 'who enter the torture-chamber of their own free will with open eyes, and place their bodies on the rack—deliberately! And yet, sillier women we, who kneel before these silly men in worship!'

Pamela was to wed Gervas, and was preparing a well-seasoned tissue of falsehoods to hold her sister up to ridicule! What did it matter? She knew that he liked her not—but oh! how humbling to pride would be that tale! That the nameless one had raised her eyes to *him* and given her heart where 'twas not wanted! To a pampered beauty how humiliating! And could she deny that it was true? No! There came the sharpest pinch. It was quite true! The moth had flitted round the light and burnt its wings. The kind Duchess had warned her—but with steady arrogance she had declined to see. Alack, alack! She saw it now—too late. 'You must not stand between them,' her Grace had said. Had she desired to stand between? Not knowingly. If he loved that base girl, let him take her and be happy! Then with rising self-contempt she felt he would be wretched, an that she would be glad of it. How mean and low! 'In my inmost soul I long for his undoing—much I must love him then!' she pondered. And that other news, which had been the *coup de grâce*.

Lord Belvedere, without a word of warning, had

promised her to Crump! By what right? What prodigious impertinence! Was she, who had been the accepted goddess, with all London grovelling at her feet, to be suddenly taken possession of by a despicable old pantaloon whom, until lately, she had never seen, and given irresponsibly away to the *premier venu*, like a bit of cheese? Talk of white slaves, forsooth!

With fierce indignation Bab rose up, determined to favour her papa with some such passage of arms as he had recently enjoyed with Pamela. She would give him a piece of her mind, which should serve for good and all. Anything like the presumption of the men, who think that women were made to walk chained and gagged in the procession of their triumph! But she, Bab, would let him know that her place was in the chariot, not marching by its wheels.

And Crump, too! The man who had insulted her on the night of her party, who had candidly admitted having fought against his love. Crump, whose shilly-shally wavering and inexplicable indecision had turned her indifference into dislike, and a settled resolve never to hearken to his pleading. And now—without being in anywise consulted—to be quietly handed over to this person—just when she had made that other dread discovery!

Never—never—never! Reviewing the past, Barbara set her teeth; and, crossing her arms, paced the room with rapid strides. Ill-conditioned Pamela had been cruel and rough, but what she said was true. What right had she, Barbara, to intrude in a house in the character of kill-joy, and set its inmates by the ears? She had no place there, and never would. She could never be more than the stranger within the gates—on sufferance. If anyone had an evil-eye 'twas she, not crazy Charlotte. And yet, she had never asked to be taken from the stage. Why will busybodies meddle with our fortunes?

Lord Belvedere had once meant kindly, doubtless; but, from his alacrity in closing with the first bidder, was clearly tired of a whim. Yes! 'Twas a whim—no more; for there was no love possible between the two. And this was the end of the dream—of the longing to find a father!

How right was the vixen Belfield! As she swept across the room, Barbara's long-smouldering resentment and dissatisfaction with her condition kindled and shot up into a flame, lurid and scorching, while a dark frown knitted her straight brows. What had she done to be so evilly entreated? For so young a girl to be called upon to fight the world alone was bad enough; but to be hampered by two despicable parents, who persisted in interfering with her volition, was intolerable. What parents! The one, a callous, selfish, superannuated debauchee; the other, the worst of hypocrites. And why had she been cursed by such a nature as was hers, if condemned to fight alone? A nature possessed by a shuddering horror of poverty; an instinctive dread of all that's mean and sordid? And what was she to do now? Obey? Never! Fight? Aye! tooth and nail—to the death, if need were.

Certainly she would fight; accept of no husband at such a father's hands; admit of no allegiance. For what benefits was she bound by gratitude to either parent? None. Both had left her in neglect when guiding care was needed. Her mother had made a lure of her—a means to line a nest withal. My lord, when he found his child admired, had deigned to patronize.

A sickening sense of choking rose in spasms to her throat as, with quivering white lips and hot dry eyes, Bab looked at her presentment in the mirror. Alone—utterly alone—beauty and sharp wits her weapons. The world had been good for a brief while; and, as usual, fickle Fortune was weary of her toy. The weather-vane was turning to the east —balmy zephyrs to nipping wintry blasts.

Barbara Philpot was not made of meek enduring stuff—to be thankful for a sunray, then bend before the storm. Certainly not. If the Fates chose to make a plaything of her, she would scratch and bite; they might break her heart, but not her spirit. Such weapons as were hers should be sharpened for the fray.

'I will go! The kill-joy shall trouble them no

more,' she said aloud, nodding to the angry face that nodded back at her. 'A mushroom skipjack, am I? A spider, devourer of flies? Perhaps. Since I must fight, I will, without quarter or remorse. Beelzebub my only master!'

A devil peeped out of the eyes opposite, and clinched the compact. Dormant at first, then worming through the crust, vague discontent and chafing wrestled to the front, forced themselves into notice.

Barbara surveyed the bubbling scum that was rising to the surface of her heart with sullen calm, and felt relieved. To have hearkened to the complaining voices which now found vent in articulate sounds was a satisfaction. Her resolution was taken —irrevocably taken; to be acted upon at once, thus saving vain argument and parley.

'With whom should I argue or discuss?' she reflected, with increasing acerbity.

Was she not free as air, to do as pleased her fancy? Independent quite? Who more delighted than the patentees to have her back again? But at thought of the stage she sickened. The falseness of that tinselled life, with its cohorts of evil passions unleashed! She had gauged its hollowness and puny heart-burnings. The exacting goddess Art! Fiddlesticks! The goddess Sham!

Disgusted as she was with everything and everyone — most of all herself — 'twould be impossible again to mouth those buckramed platitudes. Quite impossible! Invincible repugnance stood 'twixt her and Drury Lane. No! She was tingling and burning with a longing desire to fight—to revenge herself on the stuck-up pinchbeck world which treated her so ill. Was it not treating her outrageously ill to dress her for a moment in borrowed trappings, and then deny her claim to be part and parcel of itself?

'Twould be needful in the first place to earn a living. How, since 'twas out of the question to reappear upon the stage? With whom should she abide—whom consult? Walpole, old friend, would disapprove the plan, and offer untimely counsel—better to avoid it for the present, at least. Pamela had gibed about the Miss Mostyns, champion demireps, who also were alone in the world. Why should not they and she unite? Yes; that was it. She would seek out her mother again for a few weeks—the hypocrisy of that beldame jumped with her present humour; and the move would, besides, stop any action of her father's. Ladies of highest quality—even the Duchess of Queensberry herself—kept card-tables, and none thought the worse of them. Here was an idea! Why should not she and Crimp and Cramp and Crumpling set up a Faro Bank? 'Twould fill their pockets, occupy their time, and revenge them all four upon Society.

After his scene with Mrs. Belfield, Lord Belvedere,

who above all things disliked feminine sulks, kept his apartment, refusing to come to supper. The two ladies equally deprecated a *tête-à-tête*, so the three members of this happy family took victuals in solitary grandeur, and Bab was glad to think there soon would be an end on't.

CHAPTER VI.

'TILTING AT WINDMILLS.'

MRS. PHILPOT'S sudden freak, so soon as it became known, produced curiously different effects upon different minds. At first, my Lord Belvedere knew not what to think when his terrified valet informed him that the bird was flown. With whom had the wilful soul gone off? was his first question. Then, his thoughts reverting to his precious self, he felt aggrieved. Having arranged her future to suit his own interests, 'twas annoying that the maid should kick up her heels in frowardness.

'Doth not the ungracious losel know who begat her?' he grumbled. 'Doth naught become a father but forgiveness? No authority, no correction? Is she to offend, and I to pardon? How vapid! Yet she was a brilliant creature whom one could not but admire; and 'twas just like that foolish, stupid, insolent Pamela to make yet further mischief. What have I done,' groaned my lord, for the hundredth time, 'to be clogged with such offspring?'

Wayward and independent by nature and education, Bab was doubtless annoyed by some blunt statement of her sister's—some malicious lie. Sure she would not thus run off because her hand had been promised by her parent? 'Twas but a tantrum, and by-and-by she would return.

This view of the matter did not at all suit Mrs. Belfield, whose heart beat with exultation when she realized the enemy's defeat. Return? Never, if Pamela could prevent it. The kill-joy had shut the door upon herself; it must be the business of her dear sister to secure it with bolts and locks.

Forcing her unwelcome presence one day upon my lord, she announced demurely that there was news of the mountebank. She was not, thank goodness, quite so abandoned as had at first appeared. At present, she was not dwelling with any man, but had gone to abide with her mamma.

The shot went home.

'What!' shrieked Lord Belvedere. 'The ungrateful irreclaimable baggage!'

The one person with whom Barbara had been solemnly forbidden to hold intercourse was Madam Walcot. 'Twas no freak, then; but a deliberate graceless flying in the face of authority. My lord was furious.

'*Une Bohémienne aux bouts des ongles!*' he muttered,

with a coruscation of expletives; and, shutting himself up among his periwigs, pampered his rage, and nursed his disappointment.

With a show of artless dismay, Mrs. Belfield informed Mr. Crump, when he galloped to Bushey to inquire into the truth of the rumour, that 'twas all her fault—alack, alack! Who could have guessed that the girl so loathed Sir Robert's secretary? Her innocent and loving sister Pam had told her as a pleasant surprise that Mr. Crump had formally proposed in decorous fashion to her father, and been accepted; and, instead of weeping tears of joy, she had rushed about like a fury, vowing that if she must go to church it should be in a coffin. Kind Mr. Crump must be indulgent to the poor misguided spoilt thing, since purses may not be made out of sows' ears.

Honest Jack turned red, and abruptly went his way. So 'twas irreducible dislike of his person that had caused the uproar? And yet he was not uncomely or misshapen; while as for his fortunes, they were improving. He rode moodily back to town, more resolved than ever that she should be his some day.

'Barbara Philpot shall be mine—I swear it!' he cried aloud, lashing his astonished quadruped. 'Woe to her if she be over-obstinate; for moderate delay increases hunger, but over-fasting palls the appetite!'

Barbara's friends had cause for uneasiness, for, in truth, she suddenly appeared to be another woman; and none possessed the key to the metamorphosis. The change, indeed, had been gradual, though unperceived. The slow growth of the canker that had been gnawing at her heart, embittering the sweetness of her nature, caused its stealthy advance to pass unperceived.

On the top of other disappointments it had burst on her with appalling and humiliating suddenness that her proud heart had escaped unawares, had fluttered to a shrine already occupied, had been bestowed upon one who would only spurn and fling it back at her.

Haughty always, and undisciplined, with no staff whereon to lean, she reeled under the shock. And promised, too, to Crump—culminating outrage!

The fountain of tears was dried by a feeling of rebellion against unmerited disaster. If the world had been kind, so would she have been. But the world was harsh and cruel and unjust. Out on it! 'Twixt it and her war was to be waged henceforth.

Packing her valuables—jewels, laces—in a bundle, she turned her back on the dreary Bushey villa, and fairly took away the breath of her mother by quietly emerging from a hackney-coach at the door of the Richmond toy-shop.

Since Bab had become a fine lady Madam Walcot

had returned to her old home, and had purged herself of the contamination of the theatre by the warbling of many hymns. But somehow, although she sat again in the seat of the self-righteous, trade was not benefited thereby, however much her soul might be.

The sparks about the Well cared not to gaze on elderly madam's virtue, came no more to purchase useless knickknacks, or loll *en déshabillé* in the back-shop. Dark, bewitching, scornful Barbara was no longer there to crumple them up with gibe and repartee, to walk with dainty tread over their forms as they abjectly prostrated them; and madam was secretly annoyed with herself for her folly at that supper-party.

Hymns fill no stomachs. As we descend the hill, the fleshpots from fascinating luxuries become ranged among life's necessaries. 'Tis shocking to have one's offspring on the stage, no doubt; but bank-bills and costly gifts are not without a charm.

'Twas with unfeigned delight, therefore, that Madam Walcot embraced her child, and Barbara would possibly have been melted by the genial welcome, if she had not already tasted of her mother's hypocrisy, and perceived at once her motive for the welcome.

Old times were come again, chirped the dame. The darling girl had thought better of her unkind desertion; the past should be forgot, and ties of ancient affection be renewed.

But Bab, sore and disgusted, bluntly cut her mother short.

'The past may never come again,' she said curtly. 'I am here for a few days if you will have me. If not, I will be off at once.'

Harsh and undutiful, but no matter. Do not our parents always love us better than we them? Madam Walcot was proud of so fine an occasion for a display of the Christian virtues.

'Pho!' scoffed Barbara, 'we are not undutiful if we can help it; if we can't, sure 'tis not our fault.'

This was very bad. If not to stay, why come at all? for 'twas certain that the visit could not be approved by my lord, who was a son of Belial. What were the maiden's plans? 'Twas to be hoped she had done with mumming?

'I am going to set up for myself in town, and enjoy life,' the girl said, with calm effrontery. 'Perchance the Miss Mostyns will unite with me. We will set up a Faro Bank, and fleece the quality.'

Madam Walcot sat with sleek hands folded in her lap in speechless consternation. The wench was mad. Live with blacklegs and demireps! What was the theatre to this? So young and lovely, and so wicked! Her father's child. True daughter of that son of Belial.

Perceiving the maiden's mood, the dame had the

wit to refrain from preaching, contenting herself with a sad murmur like the fretting of the sea. 'So long as you please to stop you will be welcome,' she sighed. 'Madam Rich and I will pray for you.'

If Bab had ever thought of dwelling permanently with her mother again, the idea would have been quickly discarded. The act of tearing the mask from her own visage had not improved the old lady; neither had the necessity of making her own toilsome way, unassisted by a beautiful decoy.

A poor gentlewoman hath many slights to bear. The shop not proving so lucrative as of yore, she strove to increase its allurements by the addition of an ordinary, at a moderate rate; but the beaux declined to accept elder wine as hermitage, or to believe that a gammon of bacon was a Bayonne ham sent specially by a grateful young nobleman on his polite tour. Moreover, as Bab was not long in discovering, the disappointed lady applied sometimes for consolation to strong waters, as blighted people will, which habit growing on her, she was wont to appear at dinner-time exceedingly disordered, and consequently incautious.

With wrath Mrs. Philpot beheld one day the stalwart figure of Honest Jack hanging about the Green, and presently surprised the tail-end of a colloquy, wherein Jack was heard to say, 'Keep watch over her. On my honour I promise to pay handsomely.' To which the old lady sneered, 'I know your sham promises too well, and respect your honour too highly to have it left in pawn.'

What could be the meaning of Jack's attitude? Her mother was in his pay, then? For years he had hovered, pretending furtive love; then had come that audacious night-visit at the Lock of Hair; then retreat and bootless sighs; then a demand in form; and now he was suborning her mother secretly. Even had her heart still been her own, how could she give it to a man who was so crooked and mysterious in his infirmity of purpose? No. Whate'er befell, she would not be Madam Crump; and since he was trying to work on her through Madam Walcot, 'twould be well to depart forthwith.

Crimp, Cramp and Crumpling were delighted with Barbara's proposal. 'Twould be delicious to establish *petits soupers*, to gather round the board all that was gay and glittering, and as sinful as possible, and, turning night into day, live instead of vegetating. But there were difficulties which doubtless dear Bab, whose brains and energies were sufficient for the whole party, would easily get over.

The Mostyn ladies were fain to let their dear friend know that they lived above their income, including what they made at cards. Hence they possessed no available sum for preliminary outlay; and to ensure success there must, at the start, be no signs of cheeseparing. With a harsh laugh the ex-Diva vowed it mattered not. She had thought it out, and perceived that unless a house was to be divided against itself, 'twas clear there must be one mistress. She would be that mistress, and the Mostyns should give their countenance and make the evenings lively. More than that she would not exact from them. A young and beautiful actress of renown could not be without many followers. Old flames would come forward and help. Moreover, had she not from time to time received many gifts of jewellery? The costly tokens should go to the hammer. By-and-by, when money poured into the bank, they could be re-purchased, or new ones bought. Meanwhile, loveliness must be sufficient to itself, unadorned by diamonds.

To fevered blood inaction is madness, and Bab was burning for the battle. When fashion returned to town for the winter season, yearning for some fresh excitement, the welcome news spread like wildfire that a star had risen in their midst again, the brighter for eclipse, who was to kill the laggard hours more effectively than in the past. Mrs. Philpot had been delightful, writhing in agonies upon the boards; how much more delicious in a sumptuously appointed mansion, with the incomparable Gounda for her own private cook!

Sure she must have found the purse of Fortunatus; have dipped into Golconda. A fine house in modish Golden Square showed a face as bright with new paint as that of any duchess, its portals open temptingly. Two mute unsmiling lackeys of vast height, paired like coach-horses, stood, blind and deaf, within the hall. Half-a-dozen negroes, bought at the Virginia Coffee House, were grouped in Oriental costume on the stairs. The drawing-rooms were hung with crimson satin, furnished with curtains and shutters so thick as to keep out noise and daylight. In the Ring of an afternoon an exalted phaeton swept past other equipages, and from the triumphal car of Folly there looked down a woman, exquisitely dressed, with a black boy by her side wearing a silver collar; and as she flicked her team of roans she bowed right and left with winning smiles and inclinations, and invited guests to her assembly.

'That's Fortune's pampered child,' folks whispered, as she swept past in a cloud of dust; and, in truth, it seemed so. Past successes were snuffed out by the radiance of the gorgeous present; and people who called at the new house were staggered by what they saw there.

Apparently the Diva never slept. Though champagne-corks were popping all the night, with morning commenced a procession of mantua-makers, china-sellers, milliners, fiddlers, monkey-vendors. Gentlemen in undress dropped in for chocolate. If the *levée* at the Lock of Hair had been a crowded gathering, now 'twas like the birthday Drawing-room. And when she was attired, the Diva would go out a-shopping, in a gilt chair with damask curtains, and bearers in gold lace—such an equipage that her

Grace of Queensberry said with a sniff, 'My dear, you travel on a dozen feet, like a caterpillar!'

As might be guessed, the Duchess and other reputable friends of highest *ton* disapproved of these proceedings, and shook their heads and pursed their lips; the which perceiving, Mrs. Belfield sighed and bleated excuses for her sister.

''Tis mere spirit,' she said. 'If a girl hath not spirit, how cope with men? For both auction and play are beset with prowling lions, seeking to gobble innocence.'

The kind Duchess, who, since Mr. Gay's demise and the tangled state of politics, appeared less and less frequently in public, was much exercised anent the change in her favourite. There was a lurid flash about the dark eyes, haggard lines about the mouth, which it pained her friend to see. What could it all mean? She dropped in one day to have it out with Barbara, and was treated with such scant courtesy that she had much ado to control her imperious temper.

'Your Grace,' the flippant damsel cried, 'kept card-tables not long since, and was not too proud to pocket other people's money. Sure I'm right to follow in such noble footsteps. I love cards—I adore them—as who doth not? Would that my whole life could be one party of quadrille!'

This was saucy, but her Grace would enter a protest ere she went.

'What I do and what you do are two different things,' she remarked stiffly. 'You keep the very worst of titled company, are the prey of frippery-women, attendants on females of the lowest stamp. Having no private fortune, you certainly will come to rue it; and when you are irretrievably undone, will whine to us for succour.'

'I whine!' echoed Bab fiercely. 'I am prouder than your Grace, I warrant, for I stay under no one's roof unwelcomed!'

The Duchess rose to withdraw, but as she looked on Barbara her just resentment softened.

'Poor wench!' she murmured. 'How shall we minister to this mind diseased?—for sure it must be disease. You'll be sorry for what you said just now!'

'Sufficient unto the day then!' cried Bab, touching the bell. 'Summon her Grace's chairmen; and bring me some cinnamon water, or surfeit water, or any water. Quick! for I'm horribly disordered. What I said just now?—last night!—last year! I've the worst of memories, thank God!'

'Twas natural that others besides the Duchess should turn to the ex-actress a cold shoulder. When, in the zenith of her stage success, the *élite* had taken her up, 'twas always in a patronizing way. During the brief period of her fine-ladyism they patronized her still, for Sir Robert and the Queen were civil, and Lord Belvedere took her to his home. But now affairs were changed. My lord, rumour said, had been compelled to turn out a cuckoo hussy who disgraced his nest. She appeared no more at Court, and, despite these manifest disadvantages, had the impudence to set up house *on the same level with themselves*, flaunting abroad with as much brazen *aplomb* as a genuine countess on the Mall!

The Duchess had delivered the verdict of the quality when she said, ' What you do and what I do are different things.' Hence, though many ladies condescended to eat Gounda's masterpieces, and to appear in the saloons of Golden Square to gather guineas, they laughed at their hostess behind her back, and prophesied a speedy downfall.

But these spiteful prophecies showed little sign of fulfilment, and Mrs. Belfield was beside herself with rancour. Old Ambassador Hastang and little Lord Byron, among others, came to the front, and hovered more assiduously than ever. Hastang or one of the Mostyns generally dealt, and the bank always won. The *petits soupers* drew together all that was gay and unthinking; laughter pealed incessantly, and the sobriquet of ' Fortune's favoured child,' as applied to Bab, seemed justified.

But as time went on, and her feverish energy increased rather than diminished, some mischievous wight invented a new nickname, which was hailed with acclamation. ' Queen Beelzebub !' Sure some demon must occupy that delicate form, for human strength would long since have succumbed to the continuous strain.

She inaugurated hops for such as had enough of cards; instructed Lord Byron to purchase hunters, and rode to hounds in a habit of green and gold. As the fair vision scudded through the air, with straight brows bent and black locks flowing, and the pallid little lord scampering after, the country people shrank back alarmed; for there was something uncanny about the stern indifference with which she set her horse at prodigious obstacles, reins swinging loose, regardless of life and limb.

As for Lord Byron, that threadpaper was shrivelled and wizened into yet tinier compass by scorching spasms of admiration. In his blear eyes there was a devilish awful halo now about the shapely head. If before she was a charmer, now she was sublime—unearthly—and he was frightened of her; the which, in one so reckless and above vulgar prejudice as that nobleman, was the loftiest form of worship. Who so open-handed as Queen Beelzebub? Easy come and easy go. If money poured into the bank, it tumbled quickly out again.

Beggars who hung about the doors were not afraid of the tall footmen, for those magnificent creatures knew that if they were to be deaf and blind to the conduct of their betters, the poor were not to be dismissed empty-handed.

This was an odd trait in Bab at this juncture.

'Twas as though she saw a like fate for herself in the dim future, and wished to set an example. She kept a box for the season at Kendal House, the polite place for *alfresco* entertainment; organized expeditions to Jenny's Whim, a tea-garden for the lower sort; and roved, with a Comus following of noisy dare-devils, among the purlieus about Southwark and the Bearpit, under shadow of the Marshalsea and Clink.

It is sad to have to relate that Crimp, Cramp, and Crumpling, fascinating belles and joyous comrades, were not above cheating at cards any more than other ladies. They did not even act upon the maxim which telleth of honour among thieves; for they picked the pockets of Bab, and Hastang, and Byron, as well as of others.

But, thanks to their experience, the faro-rooms were well protected against enemies from without. There were two nimble-fingered *crowpies* to gather up the money; two *puffs*, or decoys, provided with notes out of the bank; a clerk to keep watch over the puffs; a porter, ex-soldier of the Footguards, to carry down drunken gentlemen; a captain to browbeat such as had the bad taste to be peevish over ill-luck; and other necessary officers.

This was well; but the Mostyn ladies made up for all this vigilance, and avenged the public by dipping their fair fingers, which were like harpies' claws, into the pool. Ambassador Hastang grumbled behind his false teeth; even Lord Byron, careless enough himself, cried, 'Rack me, they go too far!' 'Twas all very well to see the flimsy beaux shorn, for they deserved it—rickety dolls who required a chair to carry them to their coach, a coach to bear them to their Dulcineas, and a constable to lodge both in the round-house—but among the members of the inner circle it was too bad.

Yet Barbara only laughed in scorn when Hastang grumbled.

'What matters it?' she said. 'Such as we have naught to do with past or future. The present is more than enough; let the rest take care of itself.'

Poor lady! The present was more than enough for her. Honest Jack, who lounged into the Golden Square saloons as others did, had whispered casually that Pamela and Gervas were married. What signified even the present now, if that were indeed true? How restrained a hoop is the round of orgy! Would no one invent a new pleasure, a pungent dissipation, such as might teach her to forget? How flat and dull were quadrille and faro! how monotonous the dance! how weariful the hunt! For two pins, like Hannah Snell, Barbara would have donned a uniform, and sought refuge from herself and her internal pain at the mouth of the belching cannon.

The house in Golden Square became a curious

menagerie. So long as the novelty of the thing lasted there was more than a sufficiency of high-class patronage. Gifts of wine, and even money, were freely tendered. A certain libertine duke sent Barbara an old riding-glove upon a plate, with this inscription pinned on it, ' I send my glove as a keep-sake. Perhaps some day you'll shake the hand that used to be in it.' Protruding from within were three bank-bills for a hundred pounds. Another noble lord writ, with an enclosure, ' Here is somewhat for your fellows to pay the turnpikes withal when you please to go into the country.'

The whole diplomatic body flocked to the newly opened house *en masse;* and so often did Bab ask for a protection against arrest for some unfortunate *protégé,* that Hastang proposed to keep 'em ready written. Since 'tis as well, or better, to be dead as to be out of the fashion, everyone with hand on heart proclaimed his flame; but Barbara was in no mood for declarations. By her directions a paper was pinned on the satin panelled wall, ' informing all friends who honoured the hostess by calling that a prohibi-tion was placed, in her house, upon the name of Love or anything approaching thereunto.' 'Twas surfeiting! They seemed to think it was *de rigueur,* beginning with old Feefofum Hastang, who, being seventy, walked as if a stake were down his back, to simulate the upright carriage of youth. No. Enough—more than enough—of Cupid. Mrs. Philpot was resolved to be sufficient unto herself—as free and independent as a mite and bit of dust can ever hope to be.

All sorts of men and women flocked to Golden Square. The gatherings there were well-nigh as incongruous as those at the Bearpit, save that all were in brocade and velvet. Though, to avoid an unfriendly visit from Colonel de Viel, admission was only to be obtained by formal invitation, the necessary card was easily obtained, and the hostess standing at the stairhead made the same curtsey to all comers. Comrades of the sock and buskin presented themselves, and received no warmer treatment than the shadiest. The elder Cibber was growing shaky, and preferred his fireside; but Theophilus was often there, and, unchecked, brought his spouse with him. Barbara had always treated the venom of Mrs. Cibber with deserved contempt. If now she chose to come and stake her salary, why should Bab care?

This indifference fanned the flame of Madam's ire. Was she so mean a worm as to command no notice? Madam Theo looked round and saw how things were going, and was glad; for the castle was erected upon sand, and soon must fall. If madam, by chance, could give it a covert push, who so pleased as that unsuccessful actress? Of course, the curiosity of Mrs. Belfield urged her to visit the saloons. She and the Mostyns were old acquaintances, though they had much to say behind each other's backs. With artless giggles she admired all she saw, kissed her sister Bab, and lost her notes without a quiver. In sly asides she rallied her sweet sister.

'If you knew how stale is my Lord Forfar, and how unprofitable,' she whispered, 'you would pity me. But I forgot your partiality. I'll hand him over soon, unless I die first of the spleen.' Then, glancing around with meaning, she added, 'Not but what bachelors' wives seem the most favoured.'

Barbara, too hot to parry the insult, looked unblenchingly in her sister's face. It was true, then. She must be indeed married, or would not speak thus. Oh, honest, well-meaning, ingenuous conspirator to have been caught in such a net! If— but why idly bandy 'ifs'? The world was black; the red wintry sun was blood-stained. With freezing calm Mrs. Philpot merely answered:

'If you are happy, I am glad;' and turned her back on Mrs. Belfield.

The latter, at one of these card-assemblies, sat next to Madam Cibber, and Honest Jack hung over in attendance. From something carelessly dropped, it came about that the trio understood one another.

So long as things went on as they did, 'twas plain that Mr. Crump was no nearer the running down of his quarry than he had been long ago. For all he had said about palled appetites, hope deferred only made him the more obstinate and resentful. From the state of recklessness to which she had now attained, it was quite possible that Mrs. Philpot might ere long change her note, and cease to gibe with aggressive iteration about a ring and coach-and-six. Since the attempted abduction from the theatre, Barbara had in the main been circumspect; specially so in her attitude to my Lord Byron, holding him at arm's length with steady hand. Now she went with him whither he would; the twain rode out unattended; spent hours alone together. Simpleton! Too blind to see that the situation was quite changed. Then she was afraid of her admirer. Now 'twas he who held her in awe. Una was not more safe than Barbara with this scapegrace Leo. But Honest Jack was too blundering to perceive that this was so. Pamela, *fine mouche*, clear-eyed through abortive malice, read his thoughts and shaped them for him. Both she and Madam Cibber were of one mind. 'Twere odd if among them all they could not trip up the too successful beauty and launch her over the precipice upon whose verge she tottered.

Pamela carried home such tales anent the doings in Golden Square that my Lord Belvedere's choler grew. He poured forth on Bath post Maranatha, in a fine diplomatic hand, and despatched it to the erring one.

She had done her best to ruin him, he vowed,

for by seeking unenviable notoriety she had darkened with shame the faces of best friends. Their Majesties must think with blushes of how deceived they had been; repent with self-reproach having admitted so abandoned a slut even on sufferance within the precincts of St. James's. Sir Robert Walpole, everyone knew, was very sorry in that his favourite should fling her fair fame in the kennel. And yet how truly magnanimous were the really great! Instead of venting their disappointment upon a hapless father who had done his best for an irreclaimable baggage, they soothed his grief with their countenance. She, Bab, hoped doubtless that her parent would be undone through her ill-doing. But it was not so. Appreciated at his proper worth, his Majesty had deigned again to employ him. He was to return to his post at the Hague forthwith, and begged that neither there nor elsewhere in the future Mrs. Philpot would presume to address him.

Barbara crumpled the paper and laughed aloud. Selfish old man! How plain it was that he had never cared for her! Address him! No, indeed! If ever she came to trouble, as everyone was so fond of prophesying, she would point at the last day to her edifying parents, as excuse for all shortcomings. He was going abroad again, possibly for years. Was Pamela going too? Probably not, since she was privately married. Good heavens! what could it signify to her who went and who stayed behind, or who was privately married? The world could be no duller than it was. Dull! drab—colourless—a sepulchre, whose peeled whitening was never renewed. The monotony and smallness of all that the world can give in the way of pleasure frayed Bab's nerves and soured her temper. The minauderies and petty whimsies and affectations of the Mostyns ceased to amuse—they sickened her. False painted leering counterfeits! How she despised them! and despising, cared too little for results to hide her thoughts. Those houris were perturbed by the rudeness of their hostess. 'Twas delightful to be able to dip fingers in the bank and lord it every day at auction, outbidding countesses for a set of ornamental jars or right Nanking teacups or a rare Persian carpet; but to be openly accused of petty pilfering! How vulgar! My Lord Byron coming in by chance to chocolate, found the three Mostyns garlanded together like outraged Graces, while Bab sat sullen, with arms crossed, swinging a slippered foot.

'I trust, madam,' Crimp was crying shrilly, 'that we are persons of honour at this table!'

'Oh, insufferable! cheat!' Crumpling wailed faintly.

'All women cheat,' responded Bab; 'it isn't that. Yet what doth it matter if I lose to the knaves of my own sex what I've won from the fools of t'other?

There'll be an end of it all some day—very soon, I hope.'

The mask once dropped, 'twas difficult to reassume it; and the little lord, consumedly amused, withheld not his shafts of satire. The Graces sharpened acidulated tongues, and defended themselves with half-veiled innuendo. If the Golden Square saloons were to ape the attributes of the Palace of Truth they would soon become uninhabitable. A pretty thing for the polite world to find itself in a whirlpool of recrimination! Even Gounda's suppers would lose their charm if, whilst mumbling the choice viands, you were liable to be branded as a blackleg.

Old Ambassador Hastang began to perceive that while he was losing caste he gained no favours from Mrs. Philpot, and that the society that flocked to faro became shadier day by day, and less decorous.

One morning, in the small hours, Madam Theo created a commotion by vowing she had lost a bracelet, staring the while at Bab, who was sitting next to her. It was speedily found under the table, but the hint was not lost upon the company; and though no one suspected Bab of stealing, they were not unaware that many who pressed around the green cloth with vociferous bets were not so squeamish.

'Twas becoming that Queen Beelzebub should be surrounded by din and uproar, rustle of silk and flare of flambeaux; yet the vicinity of such a potentate was hardly pleasant to her neighbours in the Square. All through the night the knocker was plied by vigorous hands; the door was ever on the bang; altercation in the street was not unfrequent, accompanied more oft than not by clash of steel. The venerable watchmen soon learnt the lesson that Golden Square was treacherous ground, and trembled as they piped the hours. Brawlers, hot with wine and loss of coin, are best left unmolested; and the modish quarter was the resort of Mohocks.

A tall pale youth who wandered there in rags, leaned against the railing and gazed wistfully up at the windows. The thick curtains were not closed now, for those within recked little of the world's opinion. A flood of light poured forth over the way; shadows in splendid liveries flitted to and fro with trays; peals of loud laughter floated on the air, waking the knots of heavy-pated chairmen who slept in groups upon the pavement awaiting their powdered loads.

The tall slim youth sighed heavily; and plunging thin hands into empty pockets, slowly went his way.

'Always a welcome and a dinner!' he muttered, shaking his head, as he shuffled off into the dark. 'Not so! In the dazzling palace of Dives, no place for poor Sir Charles! Yet Brother Theo and his wife go there. I doubt if it be well with Barbara.'

Crazy Charlotte's estimate was but too well

justified. The tracing of this phase of Bab's career fills me with grief, and I would fain pass quickly over it. Kindly Mrs. Clive, pained and concerned, called to expostulate with her quondam comrade, and met with no less scurvy treatment than the Duchess. Wilks was away in Ireland, reigning in Smock Alley, and knew naught of it. Walpole sorrowed over the doings of his little Whig; but when urged to exert his influence, shrugged his fat shoulders.

'He lacketh judgment who placeth a finger 'twixt bark and tree,' he said. 'She is self-willed. 'Tis a moral fever, whose cause I know not, and will pass. Then will be the time for succour.'

This sentiment did not please Honest Jack, who watched with a grim patience worthy of a better cause. The Fates were playing into his hands. No call for ring or parson soon. She would be glad to be pulled out of the mire at a lower price; and then—and then would come his moment of victory.

After a while the neighbours lost patience and complained. The Countess of Tattletongue, who abode next door, lifted up her voice and howled. What right had a hussy to perch among the *élite* and make a Bedlam of the modish quarter?

The Mostyns, after that quarrel about cheating, perceived that fellowship with Bab was seriously injuring their battered reputations. Moreover, the class who gobbled Gounda's dishes now were not prolific as milch-cows.

To flirt with bewitching handsome malefactors at the public gatherings of Kendal House was a different matter from meeting them hob and nob on your own ground. To mulct careless noblemen of spare cash is not at all the same thing as a party of hazard with professional cheats who bleed *you*. The original position was reversed. Madam Cibber openly stated now in the Covent Garden green-room that Mrs. Philpot's establishment was a den of thieves, and the attendant sparks who had burned their fingers were aware that it was so. At this rate Colonel de Veil and his constables would be in soon, and then what an *esclandre!* It behoved battered demireps to save their shreds of reputation, and like rats to scuttle while there was yet time.

Mesdames Crimp, Cramp, and Crumpling therefore chose their opportunity, and brought the long-gathering series of disagreements to open rupture. In a glib shrill chorus they gave Mrs. Philpot a bit of their mind, fluttered virtuous skirts, and told all whom it concerned to be careful about low friendships.

It was more than a year since the establishment had been opened, and during all that time expenses of every kind had been borne by Barbara. When the Mostyns went cackling away, she began to reflect. Wherein had she hitherto been profited by flinging the gauntlet in the world's face? Was it not the ancient tale of the pipkin and the iron pot? If she chose to ruin herself body and soul, what would Society care? Who but herself would be the loser? And why had she done this thing? To revenge herself in some vague way upon a man who loved her not. The less he cared for her, the less would he be interested in her ruin. What could it signify to him? He would only remark that his bad opinion of her was fully verified. And besides, nobody knew or ever would know the cause of her strange conduct! Pride had kept that secret double locked within her breast—so carefully concealed that no skilful autopsy could reveal its presence.

And now I must e'en pause for an instant to moralize. How many men—how many women—have done strange, wild, incomprehensible things in throes of love-yearning (not far removed from madness) for the sake of those who never wist of it? If we are to stand and hear confessions at the last day, what marvellous revelations will amaze us—faltering tales of how such a maid dwindled and died, withered by a love-blast for yonder unconscious man, who, hearing, stands surprised.

Chafing under the burthen of a life whose prizes were foolish baubles, Mrs. Philpot had deliberately thrown them all away; had discarded her reputable friends, had plunged into a career which never interested her. Out of sheer bravado she had gone deeper and yet deeper, to find that the lower she sank the heavier grew the unrest with which she vainly struggled. Even the blacklegs, seeing that pigeons grew shy, deserted the saloons.

She was left in solitude, with her own thoughts for company—not quite in solitude, though. There were bills in heaps unpaid; and soon the knocker throbbed with a new and different rat-tat.

'Over ears in debt,' she mused bitterly. 'So was Julius Cæsar, who, when he owed them, was indifferent to paltry counters!' But whatever may have happened in that hero's case could be of little consolation to Barbara. He had been dead and buried many centuries. Why was she not dead and buried? She soon had as many duns in her antechamber as a poet on the fourth day of his new comedy! Aye, and clamorous ones too, who declined to be persuaded or beguiled. The tall footmen, no longer blind nor deaf, swept the tables of their costly knick-knacks and decamped.

Whither was she to turn in such a quandary? To the Duchess? to Walpole? to her father? No; a thousand times no. All that was left was independence; so to that she desperately clung. Having made her bed she would lie on it, with obstinate pride for a pillow.

With an air of stoic calm she sat in the empty drawing-room, revolving possibilities in vain, while shadows lengthened in the square without, and day gave place to twilight.

My Lady Tattletongue, peeping over her blind, surveyed the once-decorous square, and retired satisfied. There are limits to all things terrestrial, and 'twas evident that the disreputable house next door would soon close its doors and shutters. The passing milkmaids, pattering on pattens, paused to knock off the mire from the iron rings against the posts, and looked up fearfully. They had marvelled at the splendour of that mansion; now dusky-winged Misfortune hovered almost visibly. Knots of men in broadcloth stood in groups consulting with lowering visages, and thumbs pointed from time to time at the dumb house which was so irresponsive to their clatter. 'Twas idle to knock, for there seemed to be none to answer. Yet would they try once more. Another rat-tat!

'Alack! How they waste their time!' laughed the solitary inmate. 'How can one bestow that one hath not to give? Stay! what noise was that? Insolents! had they dared to break the doors? It must be so; and yet who would presume so far?'

Some one was forcing his way into the very room. Mrs. Philpot rose in anger, but rough words died upon her lips—'twas the well-known figure of Crump which darkened the doorway. Had Sir Robert heard?—he always was so generous. Although she could not ask, yet if he came forward—and after all he owed his liberty, perhaps his life, to her. No. For that he had paid a thousand pounds, and they were quits.

Mr. Crump was come upon his own account, he explained. 'Twas ill-bred after what had passed; well-meant, perhaps, if not quite delicate. Honest Jack was full of condolence. 'Twas most unfortunate! He was not rich, and since he could not pay would not presume to ask the extent of the lady's liabilities. But under cover of the night, she might follow the example of the men-servants, and vanish, taking what was left. For a small sum on account, he explained to ears that heard him not, the creditors would unite in signing a letter of license —if it was understood that their prey was gone— whereby they would undertake to keep quiet, on the promise that their bills would be met in full at some later time.

By a curious and most fortunate coincidence, Honest Jack had recently acquired a little box, snugly nestling among some trees in rural Kensington, which was quite at her disposal as a refuge. An old woman lived there and kept house for him, who, having passed many years upon this globe, knew better than to ask idle questions. Marriage, as my Lord Byron was always saying, is but a musty affair—the pleasure of poor folks, who cannot afford variety. She, the beautiful Bab, who had been unlucky, might trust in a slave whose devoted attachment had been proved. He would make her happy; and, after the scandal had blown over, she would bloom forth again——

Honest Jack looked up, stammered, and sheepishly twirled his hat between his hands. Barbara, with flushed cheek and flashing eye and widely-distended nostril, had drawn herself up to her full height, and was pointing with imperious finger at the door. How lovely was she thus—a baleful Mænad, splendid in quivering wrath! Her blood-red sacque, with its ample train of thickest silk, rustled like aspens in a breeze as she vibrated with indignation. How magnificent was the turn of the long neck; the heave of the palpitating bosom; the straight sharp line of lowered brows; the imperial majesty of the scornfully-set head, with its heavy crown of black unpowdered hair; the pose of the classic arm!

'So glorious a devil is worth the winning and the wearing!' ejaculated Mr. Crump.

'Go!' was all she said, in hoarse, veiled accents; ere, ringing the bell with violence, forgetting that the footmen had departed, she swept out of the room.

Superb, most regal Queen Beelzebub! Honest Jack was abashed, shaken by a whirl of longings that scattered prudence to the winds.

'Barbara, you are in error!' he cried, striving to follow. 'I did not mean——' but the key turned in the lock, and he hammered bootlessly. 'Not cowed yet!' he muttered, biting his nails in vexation. 'At any price—at any price!' Plunging his hands into his coat-pockets, he stood straddle-legged reflecting. 'Patience and time!' he murmured; and, with a crafty look in his glazed eyes, Sir Robert's secretary left the house, whistling softly through his teeth.

CHAPTER VII.

'ECLIPSE.'

WHETHER 'twas the result of Madam Cibber's green-room talk, or Mrs. Belfield's drawing-room gabble, or of any curious proceedings on the part of Honest Jack, I decline to be called upon to state; but certain it is that on the very next day the clamour in Golden Square rose to an inordinate pitch, and became more than usually annoying to the denizens of that privileged quarter.

As is the case with all Bohemians, the bump of business was absent from the phrenological development of Mrs. Philpot. She knew no more of the management of money than of the law and its exponents. What was that sop wherewith she had been tempted by Mr. Crump, anent a letter of license and peace? She had not hearkened, and yet a dim recollection of some such expedient lingered in her brain. Peace? What had she to do with peace?

Was not 'War' the watchword of Queen Beelzebub? How brief a reign had been hers! Her subjects had revolted, leaving her unattended on her brazen throne. Well, whatever the proposed expedient was, she would none of it, since it emanated from Honest Jack. That he should have dared—again! And yet, 'twas her own fault—result of her own deliberate attitude. As she considered Honest Jack, her asperity softened. 'Twas a singular wooing, but a determined and persevering one. A wooing? A persecution!

'Who may tell what will befall?' she idly whispered. ''Twould be odd if it ever came to pass. But it never will.'

Fitful, ill-regulated waverer! How grotesque that such fantastic visions should flit at such a moment as this across her mental retina—at a moment when even the blacklegs shunned her society! But on the other hand, there were some who sought it. Yonder, over against the railings, was Mr. Deard the jeweller, usually so obsequious, who, perceiving the lady at the casement, dared to shake his fist. Unmannerly brute! There must be a reason for this incivility. Mrs. Philpot beckoned him up, and reasoned. Who had set this pack of ignoble hounds yelping at her heels? For the moment the well was dry. In any case, sure no lady could pay if every paltry person to whom she owed a sixpence came clamouring at once in a body.

'Madam,' replied the blunt jeweller, 'if you can't pay for your transgressions like the rich, you must suffer for 'em like the poor. Find us good security, and we'll meet you; but, to be plain, those who've been in and out, of late, smell of the house-sickness and smack of Tyburn-tree. Do not suppose that lurking here you will be safe; for, as you know well enough, we've only to claim the broad seal, and break lawfully into the house and take you.'

With this Mr. Deard bowed stiffly and retired, and was seen haranguing an eager circle of tradesmen, who cried 'Shame!' 'Twas serious, then. Which way to turn—to whom apply? The stage? The Diva had promised herself never again to don the tinsel trappings; and yet, in an emergency—— Then she reflected with misgiving that even if she would 'twould be impossible at present. The season was half over; the companies of both patent houses complete. Perhaps if she gave her word for the next season the patentees would allow a benefit? A tacit surrender, after vowing to fight to the death! How humiliating! No one to consult with—not a single friend.

Barbara was nonplussed by the suddenness of the disaster. To sally forth now would be to court insult. She would lie perdue all day, and under cover of night go down to Drury Lane. Perchance Wilks was back, or some one who would at least advise and guide her inexperience.

Heavens, what a day! Like a bad dream. She tried to read, and flung the book aside. What were the woes of mimic heroines to her own state? So sordid and unromantic a condition was this which had swooped upon the toast of the town, that she sat wondering, half concealed by a curtain, as she watched the storm without. 'If we get the broad seal we can break in,' the rude jeweller had stated. Each impatient rat-tat throbbed upon her brain, till, from sheer nervousness, she could have screamed aloud. What if they broke in? 'Twould end it. And yet, if she could only get to Drury Lane, something might be arranged. Not a soul to speak to. The serving-men, down to the scullion, had apparently all fled. The terrified wenches were cowering in a garret, as if expecting earthquake. Bab almost felt inclined to join them, if only to hear a friendly voice. But would their voices be friendly—not tuned to upbraiding and offence? How empty the saloons looked, where she and the Comus following had vied with each other in misconduct—setting at defiance social tenets, effacing landmarks! Sure there must be death in the house, so unnaturally still was all within, while a tempest stormed without. She was not living Barbara, but a ghost—a disembodied soul which had been freed, but, unworthy of soaring heavenward, was condemned to linger and brood like an unwholesome miasma over corrupt and tainted waters. Presently she would find her corpse laid out in some unconsidered corner—or not laid out, since there was none to minister.

Such fancies were morbid; and Mrs. Philpot bestirred herself to find an occupation to cozen the laggard hours. In the gloaming she must go, never to return—whither? 'Twas of little consequence, so that ere the gathering storm burst she could find a retreat. What should she take? When once before she crept out of a house—the damp Bushey villa—she had packed in a bundle lace and jewels. There appeared to be none now to take. Opening drawer after drawer she found them empty, and smiled to consider the ways of lacqueys. So dumb, so deaf, so stony; yet could they see, much plainer than their wilful mistress, the hurricane's approach.

'Twas with a shocked, bewildered astonishment that Barbara considered her situation. Sure 'twas yesterday that these halls were so full you scarce could move or breathe! Where were those who had laughed, and drank, and diced, and danced, *à veste deboutonnée*, as the French have it? Retreated out of sight, leaving her whom they had called ' leader ' high and dry upon the mud. What a surging uproar! Would it never cease? How slow the march of Time! 'Twas urgent to escape from the yelping of these curs, for to pass such another day would be impossible.

At last! The sun went down; the thunders

on the knocker ceased. Mrs. Philpot, with a last look at the gay silken panels, stole with guilty step out of her dwelling; and, closely muffled in a plain cardinal, hastened to seek a chair. A common hackney-chair, redolent of uncleanly straw. How different an exit this from the usual airing in a gold sedan, with flambeaux-bearers and running footmen! Through miry by-ways it swayed along towards the hilarious neighbourhood of Covent Garden; and, besides the steady tramp of the Irish bearers, their fare grew conscious of another step —uncertain, shuffling; or was it fancy? No. A mean-looking fellow was running by the side—a link-man, probably; possibly a wayfarer moving with her equipage for protection, since footpads lurk about these alleys.

Presently he tapped against the front window, and when she let down the glass, flung a paper on her lap.

'What is this?' she asked.

'A writ for £200 at suit of Deard and Lazarus. The chairmen would be good enough to change their route,' he added, 'and follow to a certain house in Skinner Row.'

A prisoner! Roused by a sense of danger of which she was too ignorant to gauge the extent, she called imperiously to the chairmen to go on. 'To the stage-door of Drury Lane!'

One of the bearers stood irresolute; the other

took off his wig and scratched his shorn pate with a whimsical smile.

'At your peril,' said the bailiff. 'I've orders to take her straight to Skinner Row. Once there, she may doubtless find a messenger.'

'Well, if your honour says so—needs must when the devil drives,' grunted one bearer.

'Ne'er fret,' said the other soothingly, as he fitted the pole-ends in the straps again. 'Many a player, I warrant, hath been in limbo, and will be again; and none the worse! With such a winsome face, sure many a spark will gladly pay for you.'

Poor Barbara! She raised the glass with steady hand, and, choking, resigned herself to Destiny. To be consoled by a common chairman! Suppose that, obedient, they had carried her to Drury Lane. What then? The patentees were changed. Old Colley had long since retired; Wilks was still in Ireland, no doubt, since she had heard or seen naught of him. Was she to rush upon the familiar boards, and dishevelled, cry to the pit, 'You used to hang upon my lips—oh, rescue me!'

Low she might have fallen, but not so low as that; and please God, come what might, she never would. No. Rather perish first.

The head that lay back on the coarse cushions in the dark might have been marble, so colourless was the face. The blood had ebbed out of the shapely hands, so tightly clenched they were. The dry eyes glittered. The bosom heaved in stormy spasms, but no sound issued thence.

Arrived at a shambling alehouse, supported by heavy beams lest it should fall into the thoroughfare, in neglected Skinner Row, the top of the chair was raised by the good-natured Pat, who nodded his approval with experienced eye.

'Game,' he grunted. 'I'll take your message, missis, for a groat.'

But Barbara took no heed of him. The stately woman who emerged with steady step was unnaturally pale, with a composed dignity which enforced homage.

'New to it, poor soul!' the chairman grumbled to his mate. 'Come on, we'll give her the jaunt for nothing. Mayhap she'll be soon in collar, and pay us double for the compliment.'

Bab's spirit was numb under the blow, for she little by little began to realize for the first time the width of the vacuum she had fashioned for herself. Oh, the first symptom of loss of liberty! the first trace of the cage! The first sound of shooting bolts behind your back, the first scraunch of heavy keys, sends a startled twinge of shuddering horror through the veins. However bewildered you may be, a vague apprehension forces itself upon the mind as to how long the incarceration will endure. Some trip jauntily into a sponging-house; 'tis only till to-morrow; and as morrow follows morrow they sink gradually into apathy. Some fling their faces on the dirty table, with its greasy beer-rings, and sobbing, groan for those without who, breadless, are left without a shelter. Some accept the inevitable with a sombre despair that makes no plaint, too profound is it for utterance. Solitary, deserted quite, there is none to think of but themselves, nothing to consider but the boundless blank of individual misery.

The keeper of the shabby place in Skinner Row reckoned up the new arrival in a twinkling. Young, beautiful, well-dressed, refined in manner and appearance. To such he was always gallant. The lady would like a private room—of course she would—a lovely room on the first landing just vacated. Would she like a message carried? No? Not till the morning. Mighty considerate, for all the banks were closed; and untimely messages are worriting. Supper? Your honour's honour will not be offended, he said, behind his grimy hand; but we stand at a plaguy rent. These poor gentlemen below (pointing to a sodden group in unclean linen) will be still as mice not to disturb her ladyship, for, indeed, the building is honest if crazy, and the shuffling of feet upon a sanded floor wearing to delicate nerves. A bout of punch to drink her ladyship's health and speedy deliverance would be mighty welcome, of course.

'Perhaps the lady will deign to ladle it!' a red-nosed gentleman suggested.

'Nay,' interrupted mine host; 'don't force the lady to drink whether she will or no. Most of your ladies drink, but some do not. We wish her well, and all we have is at her sarvice. And yet it must be confessed, as her ladyship will learn, that the more you drink the less you lament misfortune.'

Luckily Barbara had her purse in her pocket, or she might have been submerged at once under the flow of the whirlpool of degradation by finding herself in the common-room, where a bevy of drunken street harridans were already fighting in their cups. Placing two guineas on the table she bowed to the company, and seeing a foul staircase grumous with viscid streaks, ascended to the close and malodorous first floor, where she was speedily joined by a female.

The keeper's wife was garrulous, as, eying smart clothes, she calculated their value by the light of a long experience. The silk was worth thirty guineas, she mumbled. At what hour were friends expected? Was it a great debt—a real one? Dear heart! 'Twas a wicked world, and ere now good folks had been clapped up by an enemy without a debt at all, and languished till their bill for keep was more than they could meet, and honest wights defrauded. Since Walpole's cursed Gin Act came in, trade was woundy dull! If folks were to turn vartuous what would become of the bailiffs? 'Tis irksome to some to sleep abroad, she gabbled on, but my lady must strive to think it was an inn—more comfortable than most—though the bars would show at dawn. Yet was it not wondrous to think how adaptable is humankind? How soon they get used to locks and bars! Sure the lace on her ladyship's garments was worth a plum—right Venice point; and she should know, for she'd sold many a yard for ladies.

As with the greedy grasp of an unwashed hand the beldame fumbled the dress, she glanced in the new lodger's face, and started. Dismissed with a gesture of impatience, she creaked down the stairs whining apologies, and, bursting with importance, bounced into the presence of the gentlemen as they sat round the bowl of punch.

'Queer birds come to our dovecot!' she chuckled, sipping unasked out of the ladle. 'This last will linger with us.'

'I doubt it, wife,' returned her husband. 'Fowls of such brilliant plumage are birds of passage.'

'Of course you're a wiseacre!' snapped his better half; 'and yet you can't put a name to her. 'Tis Mrs. Philpot, the stage-player, as insolent a hussy as ever turned a nose up at her betters!'

The celebrated Mrs. Philpot! Sure it could not be! The gentlemen were so staggered by the possibility, that the beldame was able to filch another ladleful before any thought to stop her. Everyone had heard of Mrs. Philpot, even if they had never been privileged to look upon that much-vaunted divinity. An insolent jade, indeed, by all accounts, who had come to grief at last, as they all do, and met with her deserts! What a lucky capture! She was sure to have a well-lined purse, though unable to pay the heavy debts such as she ran up so blithely. Very stuck up she was just now, but that would wear off. And the unsavoury crew began to plume themselves, considering how they could wheedle a clean pair of ruffles out of their jaileress, wherewith to dazzle the enchantress. In a day she'd get used to the surrounding atmosphere, and care as little as they about clean linen. A clever wench, by all accounts, who didn't stick at trifles. Clever wenches adapt themselves to circumstances, and behave according to their company. By-and-by this one would become a jolly boon companion, and lap her punch with the rest, and troll a merry stave, kicking dull care to the devil. Here was her health with three times three, and a little one in for luck!

To which of this group should belong the new arrival? A certain swaggering fellow in a faded uniform blew out his cheeks and gazed truculently round with his one bloodshot eye. She should be his. Demme! he'd run the man who flouted him right through the gizzard. And so on, and so forth, until the punch was finished, when he, as well as the other rufflers, tumbled on the floor, pillowing his pate upon the stones, snoring under the settle.

There was but an inch of tallow-dip stuck in the bottle which the beldame had left above. Barbara, still wearing the same stony look, surveyed the room with a strange curl about her lips. She carefully surveyed the smoky chamber, felt the door, and finding that the lock had been removed, sat down upon the bed (for there was no chair), resolved to watch till morning. Sleep? How likely for one in her present state to find oblivion! She sat staring at the dim flame of the candle till it flickered and guttered out with a stench and a long straight rising line of fetid smoke; and still sat staring, not knowing it was dead. There was a singing in her ears; scenes swept swiftly over her brain in sickening panorama. She was too giddy and confused to think; did not want to think. All that seemed certain was that she was caged; that the battle so loftily and aimlessly begun had ended in dire defeat; that she stood in the ante-chamber of a new and awful life of her own carving, from which there was no rescue but the grave.

To all intents and purposes she had left the world, and was no more part or parcel of it. The least unpleasant point that offered itself for contemplation was the completeness of eclipse. As befitted a gleaming comet, she had sparkled for a moment with blinding radiance and disappeared. Yes. The gates of the busy world were closed upon her. What would the next phase be? The keepers of the house would of course learn sooner or later the name of their cage-bird; but 'twould not be in their habit to bruit it to the world. Were not others disappearing every day, to be heard of no more? As she had forgotten others, so would she be forgotten now. She must learn to consider herself defunct.

Although Barbara knew not the progress of procedure, she suspected that, caught by one dun, the rest would swoop in a covey; and that, so soon as they were convinced that the victim could never satisfy their claims, she would be relegated to one or other of the prisons, and languish there. The common side!

'Twas with a fierce kind of satisfaction that she pictured this, enjoying the prospect of the worst. None of her late friends would ever learn her fate. The end would be mystery. Perchance in time to come, when reviewing the history of the stage, some one would speak musingly over his port and walnuts of that meteor at whose feet all Drury grovelled; who shone and—vanished.

At any rate, let there be what might in store, to the last she would foster her pride with jealous care. She would be beholden to none. A nameless waif to begin with, she would share the fate of nameless waifs as was fit and right. It was no fault of hers—

she would go scatheless to the other life, there to bear witness against the guilty.

Her father—oh, her father! His sin and responsibility were grievous!

'Did I come upon the globe a volunteer?' she muttered, with swelling nostrils. 'Or unasked was I pressed into the service? If called, unwilling, 'twas bitter hard to be so heavily accoutred that I could not but sink and drown!'

Yes; there was much satisfaction in reflecting that if all else faded, pride remained. She would be prouder now than ever. Not a finger would she put forth; not a cry utter for assistance. What she must bear, she would bear; when she could bear no longer, she would die.

This was the unchristian frame of mind in which Barbara sat throughout the night on the edge of the sordid couch. If she might not return buffets, she would gnash her teeth. 'Twas little wonder that when the sun peeped in he looked upon a haggard face, with the devil peering from its eyes.

A grim soul-harrowing vigil! Through how many hours of dull wearing pain she sat upon that mattress, Barbara never knew. Gradually, a small square opposite glimmered distinctly into shape, with a row of tell-tale bars that caused on their first aspect a slight tremor. The dark blanched by imperceptible degrees into a cold grey—the harsh, raw chill of dawn. She was conscious of a distant echo as of shuffling somewhere;. of a snorting and clearing of throats; a rasping of settles over sand; a craunching and moving of furniture; a rustle of wakening life. Shutters grated on unoiled hinges; the hateful bolts shot in and out (paralyzing blows upon the heart); bells tinkled and jangled; there was a muffled stir and whispered colloquy; then a lull; then more shuffling and prate; then silence. The awful night was past, and day was come—had been here how long? Sure weeks must have flitted thus, or were they only hours?

The bones of the watcher were aweary with long sitting; her feet and hands were nipped and perished, and she felt faint. Footsteps creaked upon the stairs—hovered, approached, paused. The beldame, doubtless, to bring the captive food. Odd she should not have come before! It must be midday—past! Having a few guineas left, why should she be starved? It could not be the beldame, for the tread was quick, and fingers groped for a handle, seeking it. A knock. Not the beldame—who could it be, then? Not Crump? Oh no! not Crump! Sure he would not dare—would not be so inhuman as to run her down after a display of unconcealed aversion and peremptory command to go! Another knock. The door opened slowly, and the blood rushed in a flood to the girl's face and neck as with a cry she rose. Standing in the doorway with drumsticks well apart, and a mocking grin on his pale features, was her earliest flame—Lord Byron.

'Strike me comical, Bab, but 'tis vastly droll!' he laughed. 'Flay me in mustard if I ever saw aught so like a moulting rooster! Poor child, she's famished and half frozen! Hi! Hag Sycorax, stir thy stumps, and bring the lady food! Split me if the bears in the pit are not better furnished!'

In happier times Mrs. Philpot would have scoffed had she been told how glad she would some day be to see that dissipated visage. In the suddenness of the surprise she made a step forward with arms outstretched, but recollecting herself, sat down again and covered her face with her hands.

Men were all alike, and looked on the other sex as toys! Unfeeling egoists! Crump, perceiving her distress, had dared—— Now Byron! With a glow of rage she felt how hard it was that imprisonment should not bring protection! Of late, awed by the devil in her flashing eye, the little reprobate had been respectful. Could he be expected to show deference to a 'moulting rooster'?

'Oh, Bab—Bab!' railed the little gentleman. 'Where are your blacklegs now—your beloved rakes and demireps—the golden glories of the Square?'

With head bowed in shame the hapless woman

sat; for was it not hard to be gibed at with cranks and japes when your being was so insufferably sore?

'Let me perish if there's aught for a small nobleman to perch upon!' murmured my lord; and sitting beside Mrs. Philpot on the bed, he gently took her hands and strove to unveil her face. 'Wauns, Bab! cheer up!' he whispered. ''Tis plaguy annoying. Some foes of thine have laid this trap for thee; but we'll circumvent 'em. What a piece of luck! Just as I was popping on my nightcap this morning to take a snooze, there came a hammering like carpenters working on a shipbottom; and with damnation on the loons who would not let a person of quality go decently to rest, I flung up the window and asked if the house was ablaze. A friend of mine had been arrested at his tailor's suit, they said, and had sent to me for bail. He must wait till I've had my rest, I cried; but they would not let me be, explaining that they'd brought a chair. So here I came, growling all the way. And while I was settling the matter for my friend, a couple of rufflers rose from beneath the table like phantoms of debauch, and knitted again a severed quarrel as to which should possess some beauty. Beauty here in this foul place? I asked. And then the beldame, as proud as if you were her own, explained who was the cage-bird. I'd sent for my attorney to settle the other matter, and despatched him straight to Golden

Square on your account. He is below. Shall I summon him?'

Barbara was gazing through the opposite bars with the old dry-eyed stony look. My lord was disappointed and crestfallen. Was it nothing to give up your rest, to send your attorney scouring about the town, to pay fees out of your own pocket? Bab was mighty hard to please. There is no pleasing some women.

After a long silence she observed huskily:

'I never sent for you, and never would; for indeed I can make no return!'

Lord Byron coloured, and standing straddle-legged in front of her, assumed an air of highbred hauteur that sat queerly on his diminutive figure.

'Barbara Philpot,' he said gravely, 'should know me better after all these years. I could whip off a successful actress in my coach and be proud on't, since the mouths of all the rest were watering. But to take a mean advantage of a battered woman in her trouble? No. For old acquaintance' sake I'll help thee, Bab; and, unscrew my vitals, thou shalt go thy ways unharmed! Wait, while I summon the attorney!'

He was a real little gentleman, then, despite his madcap pranks and fashionable wickedness. How true it is that we may meet folks day by day for years, yet never know them! But Bab was beyond being touched by generosity. All her nature was tingling as though she had marched at the cart's tail. In a dreary, far-off way she felt grateful, but could not speak her thanks. It would take many days of rest to calm the twitching nerves after last night's dreadful vigil.

Interrupted now and again by his patron's merriment, who was vastly tickled by the scene, the attorney proceeded to explain. Mrs. Philpot did not shine as a person of business, which might be pardoned in one who was otherwise so perfect. For months and months no bills had been paid; her dishonest steward had shown false vouchers. There was, unluckily, no list of debts, no attempt to keep accounts; but 'twas clear that the roll was heavy. The plate was saved, for he, the attorney, had stopped the butler just as he was making off with it. The said plate was below; and 'twould be best to hide it, since 'twas but a drop in the sea. Deard and Lazarus, the jewellers, had pressed their claim, which was curious, for they were wont to be more lenient. But in Lord Byron's name he had paid them; so, as far as they were concerned, the victim was as free as air. There would be a great dash later, so soon as the news should get abroad; and the lady had better be *non est* before the tempest broke. He, the attorney, had made bold to send for his patron's coach, and it was now awaiting its freight.

Plans for the future? Well, what the lawyer would advise was this: The lady doubtless knew some foreigner of distinction—some Minister under whose ægis to claim protection? To him she must go at once and seek to be enrolled as a member of his household, by which means her personal safety would be secured. This done, the creditors would come to terms, and sign a letter of license whereby they would agree to leave the debtor in peace on payment of some annual sum. But this was a detail, for none would attempt to break through the laws of nations by attacking a person who was actually in the service of a foreign Minister. So long as she held his sign-manual she would be safe. All she would have to guard against would be some stratagem through which the document would be stolen, and she enticed from his protection.

Lord Byron was enchanted. Pressing claims up to a thousand pounds or so he would willingly meet for his old flame. The very man to stand 'twixt her and limbo was De Hastang, the Dutch Ambassador, who had dangled and sighed like all the rest, and who, moreover, was bound to pay a penalty for having encouraged the faro scheme.

The shuffling feet of Sycorax were on the stair as she approached with breakfast.

'Out on it!' cried jubilant my lord. 'Pho! A dirty cloth and half-fried sausage for the most peerless of her sex! How much do you charge for that, old witch? Come, Bab, pop on your things! Hastang shall give us breakfast, for 'tis about his hour; and won't he be surprised to see us!'

'My lord will have his jest!' murmured the beldame meekly.

Her bills were cunningly arranged to suit the purses of her customers, and 'twas notorious that my lord was wealthy. There was a strange mushroom crop of small demands in a long list, ornamented by finger-marks. The heir of the house, a grimy boy, was brought out to claim a recompense for having cried to break his heart at thought of the sweet lady's trouble. The gentlemen were so low and discomfited at the speed of her release as contrasted with their own fate, that 'twould be only human to supply a bowl of punch. 'Twould set them up for the day, and be a pleasant memory, instead of accustomed ale and a burnt toast. The harridans in the common-room claimed *largesse* (equivalent to *garnish* in a prison); and his lordship's purse was empty before he could escape the vultures. The keeper was roundly rating his spouse for not having made more of so splendid an opportunity, when a broad-shouldered gentleman broke roughly in upon the conclave. Odsbodikins! but he had best show manners, or there were those in the house who'd teach them! How dared he come fuming, and swearing, and threatening in an honest body's dwelling?

In sooth, Mr. Crump had sufficient cause for his vexation. What was the use of laying ingenious gins, if, when triumph seemed assured, he was to be balked? How cleverly he had wormed and plotted to bring the proud beauty to her knees, that, with the air of a prince in a fairy-tale, he might stretch forth a hand and raise her up again! She had been humbled and reduced to the fitting frame of mind, and lo! another had stepped in and carried off the prize! Gone off in Byron's coach — whither? Byron, of all people! We must admit that the intense disgust of Honest Jack was justified. What should the next move be? He would call on Madam Cibber and consult.

CHAPTER VIII.

'SPORT.'

AS Mr. Crump's private proceedings appear somewhat shady, let me hasten to point out one little virtue. When he gave his word, he generally kept it—when, that is, 'twas his interest to do so. The foxes do not always behave like him of the grapes in the story. Some perform feline feats, and climb trees to reach 'em. Although a certain damsel had been so rude as to bounce out of her father's home rather than become Madam Crump, the gentleman did not despair. He intended to possess her somehow, and to that end he wisely resolved to keep on good terms with Lord Belvedere.

The latter, through no fault of his, had failed in his part of a bargain; 'twas magnanimous, therefore, in Sir Robert's secretary to say a word in high places for the diplomatist. Not but what Walpole in his difficulties might, likely enough, have again employed that wily person without any hints from Honest Jack. But since 'twas agreed that my lord was to journey to the Hague, it behoved Honest Jack to adopt such merit as accrued from the appointment, and make believe that 'twas his doing.

After Bab's flight, Lord Belvedere was wretched —on his own account, not hers; for he feared her conduct would discredit him—and 'twas with joy, therefore, that he received orders to pack his clothes and periwigs. But what of that grisly skeleton in his cupboard, who would rattle and shake at untoward moments? What of the Honourable Pamela? 'Twas only decent to invite her company; yet with what a heart-leap of relief did her parent hear her decline! No, she said; England was good enough for her.

Ere he departed, my lord delivered an improving lecture like that of Polonius in the play. For her own sake, if not for his, he implored her to cultivate reticence and foresight. Public opinion, he urged, blows hot and cold—is as fickle as the breezes. King and Court are universally detested *now*; but for the machinations of the great Minister would have been turned into the sea long since. The Minister was sometimes popular, sometimes much the reverse; but he, my lord, was no goose, as his daughter unhappily was. He knew a thing or two, and could read the signs of the times. Though Walpole sometimes did things that drove the people to madness, *he was without a real rival.* There was the situation in a nutshell. Nobody had the smallest belief or trust in Bolingbroke, Pulteney, and Co. The Dawley junta was utterly tarnished and tainted in popular opinion, and so was the intoxicated windbag their master. Hence he, my lord, begged and entreated that in this matter she would be guided by papa. Drop the Jacobite gently, he said, and bide awhile. It is not too late even yet. Do nothing rash, and for the present don't commit yourself.

The Honourable Pamela, as we have on various occasions seen, had a strong objection to lectures. A pretty thing for the old dolt to prate so sapiently! Why, only t'other day he was racked himself with doubt, uncertain which way to steer! Perhaps he would be good enough to mind his own business, and leave his child to manage her own. Lord Forfar had proposed, and she had accepted him, and had every intention of becoming a duchess. Lord Forfar knew what he was about, and she, like a dutiful betrothed, intended for the present to be obedient. If, later on, she found herself deceived, why—the rest of his life should be made a burthen by excruciating female arts.

Thus, you will see, Barbara had been hoodwinked. Pamela and Gervas as yet were not married. Mrs. Belfield had permitted her sister to think so because she hoped 'twould give her pain; Mr. Crump distinctly told her so, for he suspected a penchant on her part for the Scotchman, and was resolved to nip it in the bud.

Pamela was sometimes satisfied about her engagement, sometimes not. It vexed her Majesty that her bedchamber-woman should deliberately give herself to one who was an open enemy of the Court. This in itself was pleasing. She really and truly believed that her father was mistaken when he declared Walpole to have no worthy rival.

'If he knew all I know,' she reflected, 'anent a certain plot that is brewing deliciously, he would think otherwise.' Then she saw in her mind's eye the day when the bells would ring, and tapestry be hung over every balcony, and every roof be a sea of heads, as James rode in state upon a milk-white palfrey, bowing to right and left, while a duke and duchess followed close behind with smirks and smiles, as if to say, 'Yes, good people, here is your rightful sovereign. 'Tis WE who brought him hither.' Not but what the Honourable Pamela, like the rest of the world, was attacked now and again by hot and cold fits. There were moments when she almost thought that the enthusiast was losing faith in 'the Cause,' for he moped, and brooded, and sighed, and shook himself, sitting for hours vacantly heaving forth dismal groans and inarticulate plaints. Was he leading himself astray and hoodwinking her? Like a douche of cold water came the suspicion, and the lady was crumpled with dismay! Yet, after all, provided the knot remained untied, were there not a thousand methods of creeping out of the engagement, should such a proceeding become advisable at the eleventh hour? Yet 'tis bad for the temper to be so harrowed. Oh for a lifting of a corner of that veil!

Among the maids of honour the Honourable Pamela was exceedingly disliked. She was so fitful and so cross, and so plaguily given to vapours, that there was no satisfying her caprice. The furniture of her apartments was never right. Red, she complained, was glaring to the eye. Green reminded of willows, and tended to sadness. Blue recalled a dear friend who died ten years ago in a blue bed. She was often caught making coronets with pins upon her pincushion, sighing sentimentally—droning till all were tired of her.

Though his rivals might be unworthy of him, they succeeded in strewing Sir Robert's couch with burrs. He was steadfastly resolved that England should not be drawn into the Polish squabble. Any question which affected her maritime interests, crippled her commerce or threatened her prestige, was to be dealt with vigorously. That was understood. But in matters in which neither her honour nor possessions were involved, she was to be held aloof from the aggressive.

Now, things abroad were going from bad to worse

—becoming extremely tangled. The Emperor of Austria had so warmly espoused the cause of his candidate for the Polish throne, that he found himself caught in a war with both France and Spain, wherein he had considerably the worst of it.

The sympathies of Britons are always with the weak; and the aspect of a power that had once been a staunch ally fighting single-handed against overwhelming odds appealed to their sense of fair play. Opposition yelled for war, and branded Walpole with the epithets of feeble, craven, pusillanimous.

In the maintenance of a pacific and neutral policy the Minister stood isolated. Was an old friend, the House of Austria, to be humbled by an old foe, the House of Bourbon? Like a warhorse, the Dawley farmer sprang up and neighed for battle. If England were to be pulled into the scrimmage, what a chance for the Jacobites! They were terrible people, those Jacobites. When the Gin Act was passed whereby the philanthropist, Sir Joseph Jekyll, with Walpole's approval and help, endeavoured to lure back the people to a more wholesome beverage, the Dawley junta goaded the mob to insurrection. Rivers of gin were poured forth for the crowd's behoof merely to annoy Government, and many perished, poisoned or shot, ere quiet was restored. Now they were bent, urged by the same magnanimous motive, on war, and left no stone unturned to upset the abominable Bluestring! And at this moment came the General Elections! Walpole was in real danger, for 'twas the old story. He was as indifferent as ever to the number of enemies he made. Even in his own county of Norfolk Opposition took the head of the poll. It seemed as if he was about to be overset at last, for in his absence even the Queen became discouraged. The horizon was black on all sides, and the incorrigible corrupter murmured that 'if growing complications were due to faults of his, 'twas because he had been niggard in his bribes.'

In such self-accusation how he wronged himself! During the last ten years the secret-service item had run up to the prodigious sum of one million five hundred thousand pounds. While the turn of the elections was doubtful he played the hospitable host; and guests—lucky people—occasionally found a five-hundred-pound note nestling comfortably in their napkins.

Most happily for him, the favour of Mr. Medlicote was on the increase, and that gentleman stuck to his colours. The Queen could not do without him. He sat with her each morning while she breakfasted, rode by the side of her chaise when she went a-hunting; quarrelled and disputed, and made it up again·

'If I were not so old,' she often said, 'I should be talked of for this creature!'

She did not at all approve of his dangling after Mrs. Belfield. 'You could do much better,' she urged.

To which he always replied lightly:

'Let be. Despite myself, she fascinates me. Men are all fools in these matters. If she's to be my fate, your Majesty cannot prevent it. This being so, why waste precious breath in futile argument?'

It sounds strange, no doubt, to speak of an elderly lady with grown-up sons and daughters going a-hunting. But his Majesty the King loved the chase, and the Queen, to keep up her influence over him, always did what he did. What deigned the King to hunt? Reynard? No. The noble stag? No. Concerning the former, he was wont to say that 'twas a low pastime for a man of quality to be tormenting a poor fox that was generally a better beast than those who rode after him. Moreover, the animal was not edible. His Majesty preferred hunting turkeys (wild ones); and, to that end, stocked Richmond Park with three thousand of those fowls. And very good sport they gave, too; for they were as stupid and perverse as many men and women, preferring to fly low, closely pursued by dogs, and only when hard driven took refuge in the trees, where, with a little musketoon, his Majesty picked them off.

Out of sight, out of mind. Walpole, in disgust with everything in general, had retired to sulk at Houghton, since my Lady Walpole chanced to be elsewhere. Gin and Excise had gone so badly, that George was somewhat shaken in his allegiance, and his temper was therefore bad. The trusty Ranulph saw with concern that in his absence his friend was seriously losing ground with the Queen as well as the King; and so he laid a snare to lure him back to Court. He reminded their Majesties that they had not hunted for some time; that summer was waning; that, since the King threatened to run off to beloved Hanover shortly, the turkeys would be left forlorn.

Caroline's favourite residence, as we know, was in Old Richmond Park, 'twixt Richmond town and Kew, too small a domain for sport. Of the New or Great Park, Walpole's son was Ranger, though practically it was occupied by Sir Robert himself as a residence during pleasure. Hence, when the turkey mania set in, the King was the guest of the Minister; and, urged by cunning Ranulph, the Queen indited an epistle one day to the sullen hermit, begging permission to hunt. 'If you are too busy to attend, pray stop at home,' she wrote. 'I will promise not to invade the bower of Fair Rosamond Skerrit.' This was jocose, but cool; and Sir Robert saw at once, as Ranulph wished, that his presence was urgently needed, unless the bundle of sticks was to fall asunder which he had tied with such care and skill.

The Dawleyites, as usual, were wrong about him. His personal ascendency was so great, that the moment her eyes rested on his fat familiar figure, the doubts and fears of Caroline melted into air.

'*Je l'aime*,' she whispered to Ranulph, '*malgré ce gros corps, ces jambes enflées, et ce vilain ventre!* I love him, but not like Fair Rosamond Skerrit,' she added, sighing. 'It must be his intellect and not his figure she adores. Ah, poor human nature!'

Ah, poor human nature, indeed! They were rickety specimens that Sir Robert entertained at breakfast under the colonnade of the Old Lodge on a delicious September morning. This Old, or Ranger's Lodge was an elegant brick building on rising ground, commanding a prospect of old oaks and a sheet of water. From its windows could be obtained a lovely view of undulating green and feathery bracken, while the sprightly deer in graceful herds imparted to the sylvan scene a fascinating beauty.

The rickety specimens of humanity who sat sipping Bohea (Sir Robert preferred sack, with a dash of gentian-root as a fillip) were not so pleasant to look upon. The martyrdom which the royal family endured would have pleased the Jacobites if they'd known of it. The King, the Queen, and the Princesses all suffered from ill-health, and all pretended that their constitutions were of iron. Only yesterday her Majesty was twice blooded for low fever, and yet the King insisted on her sitting through a long state concert in full dress, while the music of Handel and Farinelli buzzed in her ears. George himself was choking with sore throat, and shook in every limb as he staggered out of bed this morning. At breakfast now he is near swooning, but he said he would hunt, and he will hunt—for, whatever else he might lack, dapper George was not wanting in courage — with all the more go and vigour, in that the hated Prince of Wales has sent unasked to say that he will join in the royal pastime.

Walpole was shocked when he saw how ill the Queen looked. She was certainly not so strong as she used to be. What if she were to die? Who would then govern the impossible irascible King? He would marry again. Would the second wife prove as tractable as the first? With faithful Caroline for queen, and silly old Suffolk for a mistress, the Minister had it all his own way. Here, by-the-bye, was a new trouble rising. Was there to be no end to 'em? Ranulph, in priming his friend and master this morning, and putting him *au courant* with all that had passed in his absence, hinted that the King was getting tired of Suffolk.

This was grave, though her Majesty treated it lightly—much too lightly. The miserable woman had undergone galley-slavery for twenty years to an odious temper and capricious tyranny with little reward beyond abuse and an empty title. She was too stupid to give trouble. Where could such

another paragon be found? It was all very well for
Caroline to laugh and say, '*Faut se consoler de touts
des malheurs.*' Some women never know when they
are well off, and are never grateful for mercies.
For three hours every evening during twenty years
the *souffre douleur* had relieved her Majesty of the
King's presence. 'Tis ill putting off old gloves till
we know what the new ones are like. Her Majesty
was indifferent now—pray Heaven she might not
repent it!

At the breakfast-party this morning, Sir Robert's
cards were hard to play. Their Majesties' tempers
were not sweetened by a struggle with illness, or
with the prospect of Fred's advent. Sure he had
heard of the indisposition, and was coming to in-
vestigate! The Prince of Wales showed amazing
ingenuity and perseverance in ways of making himself unpleasant. On this occasion he was as offensive as ever; for who must he bring in his suite
but Gervas Lord Forfar, the Court enemy, who
recked of Dawley—who, since the kidnapping
escapade and that scene in the House, had been cut
dead by the Prime Minister. Even Pamela was
scarce pleased by the apparition; for she could not
very well bill and coo under the Queen's nose. Perceiving that he was sad and dumpish, the spirit of
mischief seized that lively damsel; and, summoning
Medlicote to her side, she forthwith launched into

an outrageous flirtation with the young Vice-Chamberlain.

'Love you?' she shrieked. 'Never. I'll never love a laced coat and a perfumed periwig. We make spaniels of such chocolate-house beaux as your worship; and the worse we use you, the more you fawn. Yet I'm not sure. If I take you for a husband some day, 'twill be to make you utterly contemptible.'

'Nay,' laughed Ranulph good-naturedly; 'I'm not in the running with your glum patriot, who holds you leashed. And yet I've done my best.'

'And had your reward,' perked Pamela. 'Have I not read your odious billets, and suffered you to gallant my fan and kiss my lapdog?'

'Alas! I'm driven from the field! I've danced with you, sung to you, writ verses on you, sworn I'd shoot every man who looks on you. I've bribed your servants, petted your monkey, kissed your black page, talked jam to the housekeeper, and bespattered reputations with your woman—and all for what? To see you give your hand to a Tory! I ask your Majesties if 'tis not scurvy treatment?'

Certainly Ranulph was always full of tact. Badinage is more useful sometimes than the soundest talk, and this was clearly the moment for it. Sure, if we persist in hunting, despite the disadvantages of phlebotomy and sore-throat, 'tis to escape for a time from our worries. No one was better aware than their Majesties that the thorns of Fred's character were sprouting terribly. He wanted money, he wanted to be married; he wanted a variety of inconvenient things, and, primed by the Dawleyites, was prepared to demand them at the sword-point, instead of craving them as favours.

That Lord Forfar should have come with him to-day into the enemy's camp, was proof that the Heir Apparent allowed himself to be made a tool for the exasperation of his parents and their Minister. The Queen bestowed a grateful look on her Vice-Chamberlain as a hint to continue skating.

'By-the-way, Mrs. Belfield,' he drawled, 'the young lady who pretends to be your sister has been up to her pranks again.'

Pamela twitted him before his successful rival, did she? To bestow a gentle slap by reference to an unwelcome subject would avenge himself and please her Majesty.

'My sister? You know I've renounced rouge, and you would make me blush—unkind!' returned Mrs. Belfield. 'Speak to me not of that abandoned one! I fear she'll soon make one of the Keeper of Newgate's *levée*.'

'Not so,' replied Medlicote. ''Tis the queerest tale. My Lord Byron it seems—devoted swain— hath opened his purse to her; but you might as well pour coin into the ocean. To evade pursuit, she flew to that hoary reprobate, le Comte de Hastang, entreating protection and patronage, which was accorded with alacrity. It seems that, goaded by some ungenerous person, a number of her creditors rushed post-haste to the Dutch Embassy with threatening gestures, which the Ambassador, for the honour of his cloth, was of course compelled to resent. A mob soon gathered, and demanded the cause of the uproar. If anyone had explained that 'twas only a debtor in sanctuary, the people would have dispersed; but a voice out of the crowd declared that his wife was concealed within, forcibly abducted by the foreigner, and kept against her will. You may conceive the result! The windows were broken in a twinkling, and the mansion would have been wrecked ere assistance could arrive, but for the undaunted and unflinching bravery of that strange woman. Amid the clatter of falling glass she appeared on the balcony, frowning down upon the turmoil, and motioned for silence, as if the crowd below had been her slaves. "That speaker was a dastard and a liar," she said. "I am the actress, Barbara Philpot—no man's wife, or ever like to be. If ye'd see a weak woman who never harmed ye flung into jail, have your will. Here is the paper that the Count de Hastang hath writ for me. Take it, and may my fate be yours!" With that she flung a document among them, from which they recoiled as if it had been a round shot. Many knew her by sight, and wist that her speech was truth. Perceiving the ebb, she followed up her advantage by crying piteously, " I have a secret foe. Who 'tis I know not; for, indeed, of my own wish I never injured any soul. He is among ye now, and told that lie. I pray ye search out the reptile!" The hint was taken; but the mischief-maker, whoever he was, had made good his retreat; and by the time a company of Guards had galloped to the scene there were none left but a few idlers.'

'As seldom out of debt as out of countenance!' Pamela observed, bridling.

'What happened to the paper?' asked the Queen.

'The fickle mob turned, as usual, like a weathercock. Amid general applause the document was picked out of the mud and presented on the end of a stick to the lady, who still stood in the balcony.'

Sir Robert looked up, suddenly interested.

'Nay,' he said, 'you are surely mistaken. It cannot be so ill with her, or she would have sent to me. Know you aught of it?'

This to Honest Jack, who had been standing at a respectful distance awaiting his patron's leisure.

'Had it been so, she would have surely sent,' he answered quietly.

'Poor Bab!' mused Walpole. 'Sure her brain is touched by some hidden canker. But if it goes really ill, 'tis time to interfere so far as her humour will allow. Heaven forgive my neglect, but I've been desperately harassed of late. She's a singular girl, independent, and a spitfire. No later than to-morrow I will ride myself and see what may be done.'

'If I might venture to suggest, knowing the lady,' remarked Honest Jack, with deference, 'perchance it might be better for me to go in your honour's name. If it should be a fact that the Dutch Ambassador hath accepted the *corvée* and acted like a true friend, he would surely resent interference.'

'Perhaps,' assented Sir Robert. 'We must be delicate; but it assuredly is strange—most singular that if in a desperate strait she should not have applied to me.'

'A very singular woman,' echoed Lord Forfar. 'As interesting a riddle as any I have known—save one' (this with a bow to his betrothed). 'To me she's incomprehensible. Time was when I thought badly of the maiden. Then I knew I was wrong, and could not but admire such fearlessness—such activity and energy. Then came this deplorable backsliding, which, as Sir Robert hints, must be a phase of madness. She is a sphinx. I would myself gladly assist her if I might.'

Mrs. Belfield's complexion turned to a green hue that was unbecoming, as she exchanged glances with the secretary.

Meanwhile, his Majesty grew restless; for the sun

was rising in the heavens, and a long string of carriages and horses were parading on the road hard by. Fred, too, was coming to open quarrel with his sisters, who refused their coffee because he had bidden his own servant to pour it, and they dreaded some covert insult. Were not he and they always battling over etiquette? When they went to dine with him, did they not frequently find stools placed for them at the table instead of chairs—a device to hurt their pride? Not but what they were capable of looking after themselves; for on these occasions they invariably stood in the anteroom till the chairs had been replaced.

Despite his throat, his Majesty was going a-hunting; so he climbed upon his horse, and everyone else climbed on theirs. The Princesses scampered with their own following, the Queen trundling behind in a low chaise, with Ranulph riding by her side. Sir Robert's infirmities did not permit of firing at turkeys in trees, so he retired to work with his secretary until the sport was over. 'Twas strange about his little Whig. He could not keep his thoughts from her, with an aggrieved feeling of pique at her having applied to Hastang, instead of to himself, for succour. Well, well! Honest Jack would report on the morrow as to whether she would like to see him. 'Twould be a desperate breach of etiquette to meddle with the Ambassador's affairs. Time was when he was certain of a welcome from the pretty lady; but now, as he must perforce suppose, she was tired of him. Lately, somehow things went desperately crooked. It must be that he was getting old; and when we get old and boring, all but the trustiest fall off. 'Tis the common fate of all. The cloud had passed from the Queen's brow; that was a mercy. How good of Ranulph to warn him! What of old Suffolk? The King must be sounded on this point before he should start for Hanover. Aye, and on how many other points? Verily, he was so difficult to manage, that 'twas like playing on a harp with strings of thread. One by one they broke under the touch, however skilfully played. Would it not be better to fling off the yoke of shameless slavery, and retire with Skerrit to a desert island? But then, how charmed the Dawleyites would be! No; that would never do.

The Minister, in exceeding low spirits, was buffeting in a maze more intricate than that of Hampton Court, or of the Queen's Lodge close by. How pleasant it would be if the little Whig were to drop in as in old days and deliver sage opinions! Alas! the world moves on too fast for us, leaving us plodding behind, weighed down with years and care! Why may we not stay the turning-wheel at given points, then hurry over others? At this minute the little Whig was delivering sage orations to old Hastang upon Dutch politics, no doubt. Really, how she could! He, Sir Robert, was neither so old nor so ugly as Hastang. Beauty and the Beast! 'Twould be droll if they made a match of it. As for himself, if Lady Walpole would only die, he would espouse Skerrit. Then Sir Robert smiled a transient smile as he thought of marrying Skerrit, which quickly faded as he conned the papers which, one by one, were placed by Honest Jack before him.

On the whole, all things considered, elections had gone better than could have been hoped. He was still in power—had escaped, as the vulgar have it, by the skin of his teeth.

'Fickle people!' he murmured. 'You deserve not an honest servant! Your interest is my interest; or rather mine is and shall be yours. Some day you'll regret the useless harrying suspicion and empty jargon you've flung at my devoted pate. The King! the King! Let us hope he will kill many turkeys, and return in a more tractable mood. He must be coaxed to a better mind ere he starts for Hanover; and then, he may stay away—— The longer the better; for, with full powers, the Queen and I will settle public business as seemeth good unto us.'

The King was decidedly an exasperating master, for he was inopportunely burning for the fray, panting for military laurels; and yet Walpole stood out steadfastly for peace, in spite of all that could be urged in favour of beloved Germany. His Minister had increased the army, and even established a camp in Hyde Park to amuse his lord, just as we give a boy a box of wooden soldiers. There was no doubt that George cared more for the welfare of Hanover and Herrenhausen than that of England—so did Caroline, for that matter—and 'twas difficult to make them understand that it would not do to sacrifice the kingdom for the good of the precious principality. All this would have to be gone into so soon as the hunt was over. George must be told roundly that if he would mix himself in foreign embroglios, the day might come, and speedily, when he would have to defend his British crown on British ground. As for Caroline, he was easy; for Ranulph had been instructed during turkey intervals to shake the Jacobite bogey at her. The Pretender was a stick which kept her in perfect order, and she would return convinced and help to coerce the King. But Kinski, Austrian Ambassador, was also careering after turkeys, and while Ranulph argued with the Queen was earwigging his Majesty. No one hated Walpole so much as Kinski, who wrote diatribes to Vienna about him as violent as anything of Bolingbroke's. His Majesty returned presently much the worse for the outing, and worried to death by the Austrian, and stormed up and down the Minister's study, while Caroline wept over egg-flip. Was it a wonder if, baulked on all sides, annoyed, provoked, harassed, Sir Robert should have forgotten all about the absent little Whig, who had thrown him over for another? Was it surprising that Mr. Crump, knowing what we know of his desires, should have quite forgotten to remind him?

CHAPTER IX.

'MRS. BELFIELD GROWS MORE PERPLEXED.'

THE Royal hunt over, Lord Forfar whispered something to his betrothed which flushed her cheek with renewed hope, and spurred his horse in the familiar direction of Dawley.

'It's coming to a head,' was what he whispered.

Although considerably disappointed in the matter of the General Elections, Cincinnatus on his farm was radiant, as, without rising, he waved a welcome to the new-comer. In the middle of a hayfield he had just been through all the ins and outs of the grand scheme that was ripening so nicely, had weighed the pros and cons, and tinkered up the holes as Chesterfield and Pulteney touched on the various points.

We are accustomed to conjure up conspirators in huge sombreros and great cloaks, armed to the teeth, whispering in cellars by light of a flickering torch. How different this scene! A calm evening in early autumn; crows cawing home across a cloudless sky, whose blue at the edges was deepening to pink and saffron. A vast field shorn by the mower, unadorned with trees, so that the group in the centre could talk with ease without dread of being overheard.

Upon the top of a haycock, under whose lengthening shade a group of gentlemen were sprawling, sat my Lord Bolingbroke, resplendent in salmon satin, daintily trimmed with pearls; his hat of white beaver jauntily cocked. His hair, as usual, was combed off his face, and caught behind by a great bow. His vest was of silver tissue with pearl buttons; his stockings of cream silk. In one jewelled hand he held a jug of syllabub, in the other a tiny teacup of fine Chelsea.

Near him lolled my Lord Chesterfield, a laced kerchief spread upon the grass to support his diamond snuff-box, and close by Pulteney, who eagerly conned a note-book.

A picnic party, apparently; exquisites from White's suddenly transferred to the country by some malevolent fay. Not so. When Gervas advanced to greet the party, having tied his horse to a gate, they were calmly chatting high treason, arguing in silvery accents as to what was to be done with the usurper. The plot that had been so long a-hatching was certainly coming out of its shell. All the details were arranged. 'Twas merely a matter of deciding upon the most propitious moment—or to their sanguine souls it seemed so—when the bolt should quiver in the bull's-eye.

'What news of the red-faced impostor?' St. John inquired carelessly. 'Is it true he is going to Hanover?'

'Yes,' returned Gervas, throwing himself moodily upon the grass, and stretching his hand for the syllabub. 'There's no use in discussing. It must be postponed again. Sure Fate delights to thwart us! As Cromwell said, "We must await the birth of Time." He's off to Herrenhausen so soon as Walpole will let him, and won't be back till Christmas.'

There was a long silence. Chesterfield pared his nails with a gold-handled knife, and Pulteney whistled. Presently Bolingbroke remarked, shaking his fist at the sinking orb:

'For four months, then, Bluestring will be King!'

'Apparent advantages crumble when we touch them. Things go so persistently wrong,' Gervas observed slowly, 'that one is almost tempted to think that Heaven wars against us!'

'In favour of Bluestring,' laughed Bolingbroke. 'Then hath Satan won the upper hand, indeed! Oh, the people—the lewd, besotted people! His very name should set 'em hooting, and yet they grovel and cringe while he wrings their lifeblood drop by drop. We've delayed so long that sure we may afford cheerfully to bide a few months longer. Hast heard what his Majesty of Spain did t'other day? He was in a boat off Cadiz with a son of our gracious King—whom God bless—when the latter lost his hat. The mariners were about to rescue it when the Spanish monarch cried, "Refrain! It drifts towards England, where its master shall go fetch it!" And straightway he flung his own hat after the first, and all the courtiers did the like, amid a salvo of huzzas!'

'Very pretty and loyal and poetic,' grumbled Gervas, 'but useless and unpractical.'

'Hear him!' laughed Bolingbroke. 'My Lord Forfar prides himself on being a man of prudence—not like the magpie, which cannot see anything stolen without proclaiming the fact from the housetop.'

'All goes well enough, though you are splenetic,' remarked Chesterfield. 'George's instinct bids him unite with Austria, who, unaided, must surely be beaten; yet Bluestring will not let him. So much the better for us. France and Spain, victorious, will have leisure four months hence to assist their ally; and then, if things fall out as we have a right to hope, the road will be cleared for a coronation.'

'Far from things going wrong,' added Pulteney, 'it seems to me that Bluestring plays into our hands. He won't fight when his weight might turn the scale. He increases the army for no purpose, and camps the men in the Park! Thus, the bungler re-enlists and arms the very men whom before he starved and allowed to go in rags, and finally, by discharging, drove upon the footpad! They are still ill-fed and worse clothed, and remembering the past, have little love for either Minister or Government. By his own act he hath ruined their principles and made them thieves and cut-throats—mere bravoes who'll serve the highest bidder. The blunderer can squander millions in corrupting voters or bribing nobles, but cannot feed or clothe his array of tatterdemalions, who at the first brush will turn on him.'

'Whence shall our money come?' inquired Gervas dubiously.

'King James's promissory notes are as good as cash, for gratitude will be worth his while,' returned Bolingbroke with confidence. 'Many of Bluestring's rabblement are ours already; for they are not fools, and can judge that the paper of the King over the water is worth more than Sir Robert's neglect. To think we should have an army formed for us, and armed gratis, too!'

At the thought St. John was so much amused that he fell backwards with his red heels dancing in the air.

'Fools! what if *we* were fools?' Gervas said, in deep dejection. 'Although the wicked heart of man is no larger than a cauliflower, the whole world is not big enough to satisfy its lust and greed. In the history of the world, we find honest madmen and honest fools and skilful knaves mixed up in an inextricable confusion. Think of the Crusades! One of the wickedest schemes ever launched against humanity! The Popes hankered after the wealth of the East, and sent madmen and fools to fetch it. Peter Hermit, both a madman and a fool, was the fittest tool for so unjust an undertaking. Oh, my brethren, what are we?'

Bolingbroke picked himself up, and sat glaring open-mouthed at the speaker. A traitor in the camp! Their necks were not safe. Instinctively his fingers groped for his diamond-hilted sword; but, after a moment's scrutiny, he shrugged his shoulders.

'You are too honest to betray us,' he muttered; 'and yet we must be circumspect. Gervas, you gave me quite a turn, for you were not wont to jest.'

'My allegiance will never waver,' Gervas said simply. 'There is but one rightful King, and I will die for him; but, among ourselves, I cannot help seeing that he is unworthy of the great trust committed to his care, and that though we may be doing right, we may act like fools and madmen.'

What a pity! The conspirators looked one at the other, while the dreamy eyes of Gervas were following a distant crow. This man was specially useful because he was an enthusiast; and mere contact with such begets in many enthusiasm. If his strong belief in the Cause were waning, 'twould be a severe loss. He would work still, and do his best, no doubt; but in perfunctory fashion, half-hearted and lukewarm.

'Twas well for the peace of mind of Pamela that she was purring over a dish of chocolate, sweetened with scandal, at Richmond, instead of witnessing this scene. She would have read in the face of Bolingbroke that her affianced had lost caste; in his crafty eyes she might have traced the intention of warning the King over the water. The proceeding would serve to display how white-hot was St. John's zeal. Alack! She would have realized possibly that the dukedom for which she hungered was wasting into vapour. 'Twas well that scene was hidden from her gaze, or spleen and hysterics might have supervened, which would have called for pints of cordial.

The sombre mood passed off, and Gervas felt that he had been rash in speaking his thoughts too openly; nay, was somewhat dismayed to trace the form they had taken. 'Twas his turn to laugh (in rather a ghostly way); for Cincinnatus cut a sorry figure in his silver tissue in the roseate afterglow—

the Chelsea cup held 'twixt finger and thumb, and undisguised apprehension on his face.

'Our fabric depends upon the army,' pondered Gervas. 'Since the days of the Commonwealth standing armies have not been popular.'

'The people will scarce have heart to break a lance upon the subject now,' returned Chesterfield. 'They know that the House is packed with mercenaries—a sanctuary for pick-pockets—a hospital for changelings.'

'Yet Bluestring is crafty enough to make capital out of his own dilemma. He hath formed the camp to amuse the King; and will disband the troops as soon as maybe to please the populace. Without the army our fabric crumbles.'

'Verily! An icy cataract! An Ephialtes!' cried St. John crossly.

''Tis ever best to look on the worst side,' objected Lord Forfar. 'What if peace abroad be patched up before the King's return?'

'Be it our task to keep the pot a-boiling,' said Pulteney, with decision. 'The instant of the King's return must be the chosen moment. Four months, you say? Just time to prove the temper of our harness. The case stands thus: We've so many sergeants in the Park camp who may be counted on, and each will answer for his men. Is it not so, Gervas? You should have the list of officers. At a given signal, the men will move singly out of camp to a place of rendezvous, and march at dawn upon the Tower, where they will be admitted by the officer on guard. There they will seize the armoury, and distribute weapons to the lads of the Mint and waterside, who, at the same moment, will appear in force. Another detachment will march on the Exchange. A declaration will be dispersed to call the people to arms; the City gates will be shut; cannon from the Tower mounted on Temple Bar. A guard will be set upon the Bank, whence money will be taken to distribute as largesse. Other parties will secure the artillery in the camp, the guns in Privy Garden, the cannon and ammunition at the Horse Guards. You, Forfar, with a selected band, will seize the King, and bring him to the Tower, where Walpole, my Lord Cadogan who commands the forces, and the principal Secretaries of State, will find themselves already. The waking City will be paralyzed—the Revolution will be complete; for in the general surprise his Majesty King James will appear, and claim his own.'

The sun blushed red, and hid his face, ashamed of the folly of these schemers. As Pulteney glibly chattered, it all seemed plausible enough—neatly knit and welded; and yet Gervas could not choke down a rising feeling of distrust and dim foreboding. How braid into one knot so many strings? Given that on the list which he had handed to Pulteney there was no traitor, how ensure that on the given day the chosen officer should be on guard at the Tower, his Majesty accessible; also Walpole, Cadogan, and the rest? Had they not already tried to kidnap one of these, and failed in the attempt? The Minters, too, and lawless watermen of Southwark! Sure they would blab and bluster. During four long months, at least, how could such a secret be kept bottled?

The only objects that seemed really tangible to Lord Forfar's awakening common-sense were a scaffold and a block looming on Tower Hill. King James, too. How was he to be smuggled hither, and produced just in the nick of time? Why, when Queen Anne died, only t'other day, was not King James to be produced and carry all before him, instead of which he was lying, drunk and helpless, asleep among his harlots? In truth, 'tis ill serving an unworthy lord. As he had just declared, Gervas was ready and willing to lay down his life for the sake of his lawful sovereign; but at the same time a growing conviction possessed his mind that the sacrifice would prove abortive. By Bolingbroke's own showing the debauched soldiery were mere street ruffians in red coats, devoid of principle. How trust such men? No doubt nor George, nor Frederick was popular. Was James more so? Granted that the former were usurpers. A terrible blow had been dealt at Divine Right when the sacred head of Charles fell at Whitehall. Well, it was too late for retreat. The hands of all these brilliant popinjays were on the plough, so was Lord Forfar's. 'Twas no use in looking back. If Heaven willed that the true Cause should prosper, how full should be the gratitude of them, the selected instruments!

Gervas made violent efforts to convince himself, which, as is not unfrequently the case, overshot the mark. The plot must be a good plot to be approved by my Lord Bolingbroke. St. John was too clever and too selfish to make one of such a forlorn hope. So was Chesterfield. 'Twas growing dark. St. John leapt gaily from his haycock, and remarked that it was supper-time. Only a frugal farmer's meal, he said — beans and bacon and a barn-door fowl—before which simple fare the silken-broidered schemers were sitting presently in a cosy parlour, appropriately frescoed by an Italian limner with spades and prongs and other bucolic trophies.

Happily ignorant of the springe that was being prepared for unwary feet, the Court was delightfully calm in the absence of King George. The much-enduring Suffolk had gone to the Bath, and 'twas tacitly understood that her reign was over.

Caroline busied herself at Richmond Lodge, in the congenial company of Ranulph and Sir Robert, in beautifying the grounds, and studying the works of the freethinkers. She had a fine taste in gardening. Among the feathery trees of her favourite retreat were rocks and rills and cascades, chastely suggestive of the Alps; a temple dedicated to conjugal felicity, wherein were busts of their Majesties flanking Hymen's altar; while painted on the ceiling were Venus and the Loves, portraits of the young princesses. Charming! Through trim plantations meandered tiny streams 'twixt hillocks of flowers girt with emerald turf. Most soothing to a mind attuned to philosophy! But the gem of the place was Merlin's Cave—a grotto fashioned of large stones intermixed with lumps of spar, wherein stood wooden Merlin with clockwork in his chest, as true as possible to nature, surrounded by a wooden court. Here Caroline would muse for hours, gazing out at the peaceful shining Thames, discussing points of infidelity with Ranulph, wiling away the hours in grave or playful argument.

These absences at Herrenhausen were like a green oasis, and added years to the life of Caroline. No more need of cautiously trimming her thoughts for the behoof of a suspicious autocrat, of playing a part from dawn to nightfall, of curbing a temper ruffled by rude words. She and Sir Robert arranged affairs without clamour or discussion, so both were blessed with leisure, which he spent at Houghton like a country gentleman; while she varied her pursuits by hanging pictures, or planning a union of the

Hyde Park ponds into one sheet to be called the Serpentine, listening to poetry, enjoying evening drives.

But, poor lady, she was only gathering transient strength to cope with heavier trials. In due course the King returned from Hanover, his temper more abominable than before. Now nothing English was endurable. No English cook could dress a dinner; no English coachman could drive, or jockey ride; no English horses were fit to be ridden; every Englishwoman was a fright. At Hanover, on the other hand, the men were brave and gallant; the women angels. As for the queen, she was fat and greedy. Princess Caroline was wheezy, Emily deaf, Cumberland blowsy and awkward. Alas for the days of Suffolk, the buffer, the *souffre douleur!* Both Walpole and Ranulph saw with apprehension that the attitude of the King to his wife was not what it used to be. There must be a hidden reason. What secret spring was moving him? It behoved them gravely to consult. How sensible a woman was the royal Consort!

'I am fifty-three,' she quietly remarked, 'and can no longer hope to govern by coquetry. The King has discovered that I'm old. I will change my tactics—appear in future as the wise adviser instead of the comely woman.' Prudently resolved; and yet George's behaviour was so intolerable that for once in her life his spouse was sufficiently spurred to speak up and reply in his own manner. 'If you were so happy in Hanover, and are so miserable here,' she cried, out of patience, 'why not stop away? If pleasure did not call you hither, business did not; for we could do as well without you, as you could have pleased yourself without us.'

The King, trembling with rage, banged out of one door, while the Queen, in floods of tears, flounced out of the other. Things could not go on in this way. Courtiers crept about on tiptoe. Ranulph was much concerned. Pamela stole forth on frivolous pretexts, and upbraided Gervas for his want of prompt decision. Had he not declared ever so long ago that something was coming to a head? Was he deceiving himself and her? For love of him she had turned spy, and plotted and performed mean tricks. Sure he had not seduced a frail, weak, well-meaning girl into sin for nothing? Would he speak plainly, or kindly blow out her brains, or stick his sword into her deluded bosom?

Mrs. Belfield was really in earnest, and fairly frightened; for Gervas grew more and more shilly-shally, evidently had something dreadful on his mind —was keeping something back! What if papa had been right after all, and she jockeyed? Was ever maid so tortured and distracted, if not gulled? Tears and misgiving did not improve the Honourable Pamela, for her nose grew red, and emotion betrayed the thinness of her neck, while her voice grew more hard and shrill.

Gervas was very unhappy, and could give no comfort. Something had gone wrong. There was a hitch, and the plot was again postponed. Yet he endeavoured to cheer his betrothed. If St. James's were to be divided against itself, how much better the chance for James!

'Twas notorious that Caroline was the best friend of the usurper. If he flung her aside, Walpole would go too, and the irascible little wretch would fall of his own accord without a push.

With this shred of consolation Mrs. Belfield was perforce satisfied. But what was this that her lover added? If the worst comes to the worst, we will leave the country and join the royal exile! What! was this to be the futile end of it? A Roman garret and starvation! Pamela's fingers twitched. She would have loved to scratch the face of this weak-kneed deceiver! And yet—oh, agony!—it might be fatal to be precipitate. The other string to her bow must be taken up again. It behoved a shrewd young lady to hedge.

Mrs. Belfield unaccountably became softer in her conduct to Mr. Medlicote; spoke low to him as they sat on duty in the antechamber; rallied him with moonlit raillery till he reflected that pervading anxiety, while it corroded others, had much improved his lady-love.

'Marriage—ah me!' she sighed one day, with eyes directed to the ceiling, 'do we not see enough of it in this royal household? Not but what the world should be obliged to every woman when she marries.'

'How so?' asked Ranulph.

'Because there's nothing so civil as a husband—to others! He wastes all his rudeness on his wife, which begets the highest good breeding to all besides!'

Ranulph could not but laugh. A queer slip of quality was Pamela, amusing and whimsical. Perchance, after all, some day—— Well, well—there were other things to think of now.

Caroline repented the too candid speech wrung from her by worry, and resolved to try and be more patient. Yet what she had to bear was crushing. Suffolk away, the King spent his evenings in the Queen's apartment, pacing up and down, swelling and gobbling like one of his favourite turkeys, while the martyr on the rack of ennui employed every artifice to conceal her yawns.

She would drive over to-morrow to see my Lord Grantham's mansion, she observed, by way of saying something.

'Always running your nose everywhere!' snorted the autocrat. 'Pushing into every puppy's kennel to gape at his chairs and stools! Why not rush into the taverns?'

The water rose into the Queen's eyes. She knotted in silence till she tangled her thread; then snuffing the candles extinguished one of them.

'Emily!' bawled his Majesty, 'your mother is awkward idiot enough to have been an Englishwoman!' and so flounced off to bed.

Oh what a life! Cushions stuffed with pins, forsooth!

It was all very well to arrange a new attitude, to say that, abandoning the rosy chains of feminine cajolery, you will be like a man friend. Such gross vulgar ill-breeding from one man to another would produce blows. Was it ill-health that brought about the change? The royal eyes were bloodshot and inflamed; the regal cheeks puffy and red. If she could think so, Caroline would be satisfied, for there is nothing a woman will not bear if she sees sufficient cause.

George had not been back a month when he began to break the ice with regard to another journey. Prodigious! The Queen's circle glanced bewildered one at t'other, with jaws dropped. What next? Better to abdicate at once—hand bauble and sceptre to the itching fingers of eager Frederick! Sir Robert, man of the world, quick, clever, astute— who boasted that no murky deep of his muddy century could escape the experienced scrutiny of his eagle ken—cleared his throat and spake.

'No State prospers so well,' he declared, 'as one

that's governed by a woman; for behind the scene she, of course, is governed by a man.'

This was oracular, but mysterious.

'And *vice versâ*,' he continued, amid dead silence. 'Do ye bite?'

No one bit, so, clearing his throat once more, the Minister condescended to explain.

'I told your Majesty,' he said, shaking his great periwig, 'that 'twas ill putting off old gloves till you knew what the new ones would be like. The old glove was called Suffolk, the new one's name is Walmoden.'

Of course! It was a new mistress who was at the bottom of the King's ill-humour! How foolish not to have guessed it!

'What is she like?' the Queen asked eagerly. 'Handsome, young, spirited, ambitious?'

'Not at all,' laughed Sir Robert reassuringly.

'What more?' the Queen inquired. 'You hesitate.'

The Minister did hesitate, for he had that to propose which caused even his battered world-worn face to become more rubicund.

'You are prepared to act like a man friend?' he hinted, with some embarrassment.

'*Après?*' asked Caroline, with slightly heightened colour.

'Send and invite her over.'

The Queen winced, while Pamela dropped her

needle. Barbara, the now broken hussy, had been wont to scoff at her sister's conduct as sordid, calculating, disreputable. If so, she was in the best of company! To retain power Walpole was capable of anything; to preserve her sway intact Caroline was prepared to go great lengths. How great 'twas impossible to gauge. The upsetting of a dynasty for the sake of a dukedom might perhaps be contemned by unpractical dreamers as unduly selfish; but for a wife to invite a concubine to take possession! The cup extended to her Majesty was thick with acrid lees.

'*Sa Majesté n'est plus jeune, et elle en a bien vu d'autres!*' hazarded Mr. Medlicote, with an *aplomb* that appreciative Pamela could not but admire.

If only Gervas, instead of being so provokingly shifty, would—— But never mind Gervas now.

'Come, come!' wheedled the Minister; ''twill but be long-suffering useful Suffolk o'er again without her deafness. Sure, at fifty-three 'tis too late to try new methods! Tell the King that you desire nothing but his happiness—that to give him pleasure——'

Caroline's breast heaved. The wife was tussling with the Queen—the outraged woman with the politician.

'*Soit!* Be it so!' she said, with a harsh laugh. 'When your petticoat is mire-smirched, 'tis silly to shy at a puddle. *Tell him?* No; that were too much. I could not. There are some things to which even I cannot stoop as yet. He may have his new toy for me. But invite the woman over!—tell his Majesty myself? I could not; no—I could not. *I will write him a little note!*'

This knotty point decided, the party breathed again. Sir Robert, however, was still anxious; for, whereas the King would often kick while he obliged, his spouse could look pleasant while resentful. 'Twas a cruel task the Minister had imposed this time; and Caroline's smile was seraphic.

CHAPTER X.

'PITFALLS.'

WE all know how little comfort is to be gleaned from the fulfilment of our dear friends' prophecies. The Duchess of Queensberry had shaken her head, vowing that so reckless a career as Mrs. Philpot chose to arrange for herself must lead to speedy ruin; and we have seen that our poor Barbara slid with unpleasing swiftness from the elevated brow of prosperity down into the shadowy vale. Steep and slippery is the incline; seldom may the heights be climbed again. The uncertainty of when the bottom is really reached adds to the horrors of descent. She was too much afflicted to be touched by Lord Byron's kindness, or Count Hastang's helpfulness. The amount of her debts was found to have piled to too goodly a figure for one admirer to meet; there was nothing for it but to arrange the letter of license, and procure a lodging which should be secure from troublesome incursions.

The Ambassador engaged Mrs. Barbara Philpot, by written agreement, as his housekeeper, by virtue of which document she might walk the streets unharmed; but Bab's objection to abide in the house with him was fully shared by the old gentleman after the episode of the broken windows. That outrage seemed to show that some one was at work more malicious than an ordinary dun. There was no excuse for it.

The privileges of foreign Ministers are sharply defined; and, when Count Hastang formally complained, he was told by the authorities that they were very sorry, which, if fine as an apology, did not repair the damage.

In Cleveland Row, St. James's, a pretty apartment was secured for the bruised lady, where, since 'twas within verge of the Court, she need be in no fear of bailiffs. It was furnished with such articles as could be saved from the wreck in Golden Square; her plate and clothes were transported thither; Lord Byron sent some china, and three handsome girandoles; and, all things considered, she appeared to be well out of a mighty awkward scrape.

Doubly fenced round and protected, the creditors had nothing for it, as had been foreseen, but, for a small consideration, to sign a letter of license, renewable after twelve months, which they accordingly did—all save Madam Mapp, the well-known frippery-woman, whose trade was to supply the ladies of fashion and of the patent theatres with laces and perfumed gloves, rouge, hair-powder, and clocked stockings. She said she'd made an oath never to sign such a paper, but gave a promise not to push her claim. 'Not that the promise matters,' she laughed sourly, 'since the debtor's beyond my reach.'

Thus did the battered soul obtain a period of rest, which she spent in staring out of window at the bricks of the opposite house; and which, from its unbroken monotony, did her little good—for, like some distant echo from another sphere, fell upon her ear the plaudits of admiring thousands; the buzz of beaux in the crowded green-room; at the morning *levée;* the constant shuffle of feet at the Lock of Hair; the serenade of French horns; the frequently offered compliment of music in the Parks. Unbroken brooding induces hysteria, since in this world unpleasant events preponderate over agreeable ones, and the gnawing of our own hearts is evil diet.

It may be thought that Barbara was unduly hard to please, since we cannot have everything. For lack of some one on whom to lean with affection, the position of idol and toast had been as bran in the mouth, and the Bushey villa intolerably dull. If that was so, how dismal must ostracism have proved in Cleveland Row, with no company save a dog, a cat, and a blackbird—nothing to look at but a wall!

'Time was,' she told the cat, quoting from 'Jane Shore,' 'when my approach would make a little holiday, and every face be wreathed in smiles to see me.'

It was not so now. The knocker remained still, save when the polite Count sent to know how she did. Her little maid, last remnant of the grand establishment, coaxed her mistress to piquet; but even that proved sickening—for did it not recall the brief period of insane uproar—short reign of Queen Beelzebub—on which now she looked with wonder?

In scorn, mingled with indignation, she reflected on the moths who used to flit about the candle, and eagerly consulted the mirror. She was paler and thinner than of yore—no longer fresh and blithe; but in exchange for mere peachen youth was a murky thunderous loveliness, which went well with the plastic severity of the firm chin and jaw. The eye had acquired a brilliancy and fulness and a sullen depth like that of some mountain tarn. The skin had lost its roseate glow, and was now of an even olive on which the dense black brows were marked unflinchingly.

'I think I am more beautiful,' she mused, 'than in the halcyon time, and yet I am deserted. No hapless prisoner with jail distemper is more avoided. They have heard, I suppose, of the extent of my

38—2

debts? Do they think I would stoop to beg of them?'

With London at her feet, Bab had been wont to complain that, though all were prostrate, no one really loved her. That was true enough! Despite her ripened beauty, none came to bask; for the beaux, if free and lavish up to a few hundreds, had no idea of disgorging thousands for a fancy, and instinctively shrank from the sordid mean worries that come with writs and bailiffs.

The longer and more complete the solitude, the more Barbara nursed her gloom and hugged her grievances. Was not her fate too harsh? Endowed by Nature with precious gifts of charm and beauty and sufficient talent, the wicked fairy had, as usual, been at the christening. Independent haughtiness is an inconvenient attribute, unless backed by the substantial. Unaided by parental influence, Bab had tried to shine, and had succeeded, by means which carried with them their own disadvantages. Unhelped by pride of birth and wealth and social station, she had endeavoured to hold her own with the *élite;* and was aggrieved because, though countenanced and admitted into the best society, there was an intangible something which rose like the great wall of China betwixt her and the true quality. Sure she was a ridiculous maid thus to cry, as 'twere, for the moon! And what a silly creature to kick over the traces in a tantrum, and do that which could hurt none but herself! But oh, my brethren, are we not all of us struggling after that which never may be ours; banging our wings against bars; sighing, longing, hoping; building castles that will never be inhabited; weaving plans that never may be realized—till suddenly, when things seem most promising, the White Pilgrim comes and, with ghostly laughter at our futile efforts, beckons to well-merited oblivion?

A curious world this, in whose every fruit there is a worm! In which such small measure of success as is meted out brings penalties; where the prosperity, for which by rooted instinct we strive and toil, almost invariably does harm to the few who are privileged to taste of it. Why are we impelled to seek that which is to do us injury?

In great things, as in small, 'tis the principle which bids the innocent moth to gyrate around the lamp. Perhaps in the next planet, which in the cycle of progress we may be compelled to visit, we may struggle for worthy objects and obtain them, achieve our hearts' desires, meet with no disappointments. Perchance our cheeks will not be always tingling with slaps. Perhaps the dolls will not be filled with bran, the luscious apricot will not conceal a wasp, the cabbage a caterpillar. Perchance we shall not fall in love with the wrong person, or back the wrong horses in the race. Because she had unwittingly bestowed a heart that pined for the sunshine of love on one who did not want it, 'twas doubtless extremely foolish of Barbara to run amuck against the world, to assault an enemy so much stronger than she.

Possibly, while staring at the wall or talking with the cat and blackbird, she was aware of her folly; but she was not one to strip her back and kneel humbly for correction, promising to be a good girl in future. On the contrary, she only grew the fiercer, and set her teeth more sternly, vowing that if she had done wrong, she was more sinned against than sinning.

Had any of her old friends troubled the knocker just now they would have met with a scurvy reception. Though she repeated to herself that it was well to have found them out, that she preferred being deserted by those who could give nothing but lip-homage, she was bitterly hurt and outraged down at the bottom of her being to think that neither Walpole nor Wilks, nor any of those who had protested so much, should take the trouble to inquire whether she were alive or dead.

One day she was aroused from a lethargy that threatened to become chronic torpor, by the idle loquacity of her woman. That abigail, despatched upon an errand, had met Mrs. Belfield, and had made a humble curtsey; whereupon the lady, recalling her face, had asked after her late mistress.

'Late!' the wench had exclaimed; 'sure I live still with Mrs. Philpot.'

'What!—in prison?' the Honourable Pamela had retorted; 'for 'tis all over the town that the hussy is in Bridewell!'

In Bridewell, hempbeating! With surging wrath Barbara guessed that if such a report were current it must have emanated from her sister's malice. Yet who had she but herself to thank for such reports? Why mope alone in a corner with the blackbird and the cat and dog? Was it not shameful, though grievously worsted, to have accepted defeat instead of dying with a smile and front turned to the foe? She would go forth into the world again—once again, at least—and, showing herself in public, give the lie to scandal.

What mattered the sea of debt? The letter of license was signed, so was the agreement with the Ambassador. Her body was safe enough. True. She had been living on her silks and laces and ornaments, parted with one by one, and the time was not far distant when this source of revenue would cease.

The abigail was babbling still, not knowing what she did.

'And oh!' she cried, 'if your ladyship only knew of the doings—such doings!—to inaugurate the opening of a new pleasure-garden on the grounds of the late Earl of Ranelagh! Such canals, and walks, and trees, and bridges! and a statue of Mr. Handel as good as waxwork! and a dancing-rotunda as big, they say, as the Pantheon at Rome! 'Tis a pity your ladyship cannot attend the masquerade; 'twould rouse your spirits, and bring the colour to your cheeks! The Queen is to be present, and the Princesses, and all the rank and fashion.'

'Cannot attend!' echoed Barbara, frowning. 'If I please, I will attend, and as fine as any. Cannot attend, quotha!'

The abigail was astonished at the sudden change in her mistress. The cloud that hung over the mountain tarn was gone; instead, a sparkling ray played upon its surface and flooded its brown deeps with light; and yet the woman hesitated, trembled, and turned red.

'Alack, madam!' she murmured, 'your ladyship's wardrobe——'

Barbara paced to and fro, her fine arms crossed upon her heaving breast. Pamela! The wicked spiteful creature! Doubtless 'twas thanks to her that misfortune had gathered, driving like a whirlwind down a valley, uprooting trees, unroofing houses. And now, not content with what had really happened—and bad enough it was—she must spread reports of hemp-beating! The punishment reserved for the lowest of her sex! Through good or ill report, the fair fame of the ex-Diva had never been smirched or sullied.

'And more fool I,' she pondered bitterly. 'Infamy would mean comfort again, and peace of mind. Why guard my good name so jealously for sake of one who cares not? What good is it to me or to anyone? Why not rush into the street, into the arms of the first comer? 'Twould be but another item in the long list of what I've suffered at the hands of the cruel world!'

Bab passed a hand over her brow. Sure she must be going mad! Were she to fall, who so glad as Pamela? Pride stepped in to the rescue. In prosperous days she might have given herself—who knows?—perhaps; but now, through poverty, to earn a crust to stave off a day's starvation!

Mr. Hogarth, she remembered, had painted but a year or two ago a tragic picture called 'The Lady's Last Stake.' Should it be said that when he limned it, he had in his prophetic eye the actress, Barbara Philpot? This report anent the hemp-beating. Should she qualify herself for Bridewell, and justify her sister's calumny? It was too bad, though! Come what might of it, she would show herself at this masquerade. 'Twould be fine to watch the confusion of fair-weather friends! 'Twould be necessary to appear in flaunting bravery. Her jewels were sold long since, but the plate remained—had been kept till the last as a bulwark against hunger. Deard and Lazarus had behaved ill at the time of the crash. 'Twould not do to have further dealings with them; but there were other jewellers, who would lend a set of diamonds on the plate's security—a *rivière*—anything which should show to the world that the story of poverty was false.

Abigail was right about the wardrobe. Mrs. Mapp might be coaxed into supplying new brocade. At all events, it would do no harm to sound her. The frippery-woman arrived with promptitude, and was vastly civil.

'Sure, madam, with youth and such beauty one need not starve!' she said slily, with veiled lids. 'His Excellency the Tripoline Ambassador said only t'other day——Nay, your ladyship should not be vexed—on one side belonging to the quality, too. If you only knew what I know of all the Lady Bettys and the Lady Townleys! But mum's the word. I can keep my place, I hope!—aye, and my teeth closed!'

As to the new brocade and ostrich plumes, it required consideration, since my lady was so stiff-necked. With a hint, his Excellency would send round a cartload of brocades and a dozen ostriches. Well, well! No need for black looks—by-and-by, perhaps. When was that long bill likely to be settled? She, Madam Mapp, was poor and hard-working, and 'twas bitter to be kept out of her money. Perhaps Mrs. Philpot would consider the matter, and return an answer to his Excellency the Tripoline Ambassador. Ah, deary me!—well, she would think about the new brocade, and let Mrs. Philpot know.

Business took the frippery-woman next to Covent Garden, where a new comedy was being rehearsed that would require sumptuous dresses, and of course she told of her visit to Mrs. Philpot. Madam Cibber, who chanced to be in the comedy, was vastly interested in the narration, and, curiously enough, exerted her influence in favour of her fallen rival. At least it would seem that she was thus generous, for Mrs. Mapp trotted briskly in the evening to Cleveland Row with a bundle of patterns, declaring she had changed her mind, and urged the ex-Diva to select a splendid fabric of gold and silver tissue, fresh-woven in Spitalfields.

'After so long an absence your ladyship should appear with *éclat*,' she purred good-humouredly. 'Fie! never heed the cost. When you deign to settle the account, which I know that you will soon, a trifle added will make little difference.'

This was kind, and Barbara felt it to be so. Robed in this tissue, with the borrowed diamonds, she would appear as splendid as she had ever been. Pamela, with her straitened means, would perish of envy. So would the Mostyns, who had been so brutal. What would Queensberry think? Would Walpole, false friend, be ashamed of his long neglect; and Wilks, after his solemn assurances? The masquerade over, Bab would again retire, like Cinderella, at midnight. But the necessary object would have been gained. An emphatic and triumphant denial would have been given to that malignant story of the hemp-beating.

The opportunity was a good one; for popular excitement was wrought to highest pitch when the day of the festival arrived. Though the dancing-rotunda was not finished (indeed it was not opened to the public until 1742), the grounds were glorious to look upon. The Lady Bettys were there in crowds; so were Crimp, Cramp and Crumpling (in faded finery), of whom some one sang:

> 'Fair maids, who at home in their haste
> Had left all clothing else but a train,
> Swept the path clean as slowly they paced,
> Then—walked round and swept it again.'

The road to Chelsea was crowded with vehicles of all descriptions—whiskeys, coaches, chairs; while humble folk gathered on the grassy banks and other points of vantage to watch the glittering procession.

There was something whimsical about this last freak of Barbara's, which, to her growing cynicism, was diverting. To be clad like a princess in a fairy-tale, with but a hazy prospect of dinner, was not unamusing. To triumph over Pamela was worth many dinners. On her way home she would call on Count Hastang, and, whilst gratifying him with a gorgeous apparition, offer heartfelt thanks for his many kindnesses. She had insisted upon moping so long alone that the Dutch Minister had, respecting her whim with delicate tact, ceased to inquire how she did. 'Twas ever so long since she had heard of him. Perhaps he would be here at this very festival. Lord Byron, too—he would enjoy the surprise. And Crump—that hot and cold, mysterious suitor—had also (thank Heaven for that!) respected her retirement. Was it respect or forgetfulness? Would they be glad at her resurrection, or recoil as from a spectre?

The bustle — the animated scene — threw the thoughts of Bab into a less gloomy channel than usual. She lay back upon the cushions of the plain chair that had been hired and closed her eyes. Sure the period of uproar was a dream—waking presently, the familiar parlour of the Lock of Hair with its oak panelling would meet her gaze—the call-boy of Drury would knock with a new part—her mother, neat and tidy and genteel, would enter the chamber, ushering in the *levée*. Her mother! What a tale it told, that in her solitude Barbara had never longed to look on either of her parents! Even in extremity she had never contemplated applying to father or mother. A knock!—yes, a real one. Opening her eyes, her heart gave a great throb. The sinister past was no dream. That knock upon the window now recalled a horrid evening which preceded a yet more horrid night. Oh, what a night of dreadful vigil—that gruesome night of retrospect which closed the period of uproar! A man of flesh and blood was bowing bareheaded at the window, clad in showy raiment.

A footman in a livery. What meant this? A note for her upon the public road to Ranelagh? Doubtless from the unknown but persevering Tripoline Ambassador. Mother Mapp must have dared—this very brocade, perhaps—— Oh, simpleton! reckless, incorrigible fool! Lowering the glass, she was about, with hot words, to send the lackey packing, when he tossed a paper in her lap.

Again!

'A writ for five hundred guineas,' he said, with a surly nod. 'Your ladyship will excuse the disguise. On the tails of wary fowls we must put salt.'

For a moment Barbara was stunned. Behind, men were shouting to her chairmen not to block the way. The latter, laughing at the evident bewilderment and consternation of their smartly bedizened madam, drew aside.

They had just reached the Hercules' Pillars—a wayside alehouse, frequented by collectors, which, as all the world knows, occupies Hyde Park Corner. As the water of a rivulet brawls around a pebble, so did the crowd fret about the hired chair. Dear heart! unless the bearers stood aside and quickly their vehicle would be poled. The footman with the sardonic grin gazed calmly on the tumult as, unabashed, he beckoned forward a knot of men who hovered in the vicinity.

Bab's wrath was fairly roused. What next? How dared the fellow presume to make a scene in this public place! He should rue it. If he was not aware that she was protected, he should not be allowed to plead his ignorance in bar of punishment. His Excellency the Dutch Ambassador would be furious in that for a second time his rights had been set at naught.

Her person was doubly sacred, for she was a member of Count de Hastang's household, and a letter of license for a year had been signed by all her creditors. Yonder was Colonel de Veil, with a posse of Bow Street runners scampering hitherward to clear the obstructed way. To him would she apply.

The gallant Colonel recognised the beauty, and bowed low. What could he do for the charming Mrs. Philpot? Sheriff's officer? Plaguy annoying! The bearers had better transport their burthen into the parlour of the Hercules' Pillars, for the middle of a narrow road on a gala-day was not the place for parleying.

No sooner said than done, since the bailiff was agreeable. Motioning his followers to close round the chair, it was turned about, and the river flowed again; and tears of mortification rose to Barbara's eyes, for peering from a coach as it swept by was Madam Cibber, with eyebrows raised and supercilious smile.

Sure never had the wayside pot-house received so splendid a guest as presently was sitting on its lowly bench. The bailiff was sorry, and if wrong would humbly apologize. If the lady would pay the five hundred guineas she might yet be in time for the fête. At the suit of Mrs. Mapp! What treachery was this? Barbara was fairly discouraged. What could have been the woman's motive? Sure there was more in this than met the eye! She was the only creditor who had not signed the license, but she had promised. Was it a pitfall cunningly arranged for the behoof of the Tripoline?

She saw it all. Oh, wicked, cruel, artful trickster! Not artful, though, for Mrs. Mapp had forgotten the protection. How lucky for Barbara that she brought it with her! Drawing the precious document from a pocket she held it forth, and haughtily bade the bailiff at his peril to prevent her from going home.

'Your insolence,' she remarked, with fine disdain, 'hath sickened me with fêtes; forthwith will I return to Cleveland Row.'

The bailiff laughed quietly, as with head poised on one side and one eye closed in admiration, he surveyed his tinselled prize.

'Craftily imagined,' he grunted. 'You're an old soldier—a wary bird. I've not forgot that your ladyship dwells within the Verge; so I don't think we'll travel to Cleveland Row. Come, no one shall dub me churlish! One of the men shall go for Madam Mapp. If you can arrange with her, I'm willing.'

There was nothing for it but submission, and for

two hours Barbara, controlling her impatience as she might, witnessed through the cobwebbed panes the passing of the brilliant pageant. Many an old friend went by—dead to her long since. There was Mr. Medlicote in padusoy, riding with—yes, Lord Byron! Should she tap on the window and call him to her succour? No. Her pride revolted against claiming a second favour at the hands of that little gentleman, even though 'twas but to ask him to inform the Count of her dilemma.

Instinctively she shrank from the window, for a tall, sad figure was trotting past, whose aspect brought the blood welling to her face. Lord Forfar! Gervas! How ill and worried he looked! He was not happy, then, with Pamela? How could he be, since he was straight and upright, while she was so strangely crooked?

Mrs. Mapp at last. The frippery-woman stood without blenching as Barbara poured forth a torrent of reproach for her perfidious conduct. Then, shrugging her shoulders, she replied sourly:

'A body must look after her interests, specially when dealing with players. Slippery cattle! marry come up! A truce to your prate, madam, and be civil! deeds, not words! Your protection is waste paper, for your Count lies stiff and stark, and serve him right for cheating honest folks!'

Barbara sank cowed upon the bench. Count Hastang dead! He had been grievously indisposed, then, while she, selfishly moping, wist not of his danger. Kind old disreputable satyr! A vague chill sense of fear encompassed Bab, and she shuddered. The procession moving past the window seemed an allegory of her life. The chattering, laughing throng approached with beaming faces, and heedless of her went by, and showed their backs, while she remained unnoticed, gazing with haggard eyes through clouded panes, as they vanished in clouds of dust.

Of what was the woman droning? Oh for silence to clear her throbbing brain, that she might review the perplexities of her position! What was it the dame proposed? She was right in this much. 'Twas impossible to linger in the wayside alehouse—and in this tawdry guise. Already there were curious plebeian faces with snub noses flattened against the glass, eyes peeping through the door-chinks, under the arms of the bailiff's followers, as they stood a sturdy guard.

Scared by the unexpected blow of the Count's demise, and dreading something more, Mrs. Philpot allowed herself to be handed into the chair again. The respite had been short. Had she not felt that the lull must be brief and temporary? Fight against the world—fool! fool! As well try to stay with a finger the descending avalanche! What must come, must. They might bear her where they would—she cared not whither—if to an open grave, how happy the release!

'Twas with apathy, then, that she found herself again in the old room, with the coarse dingy bed, and the too well-remembered bars across the square of light. The captains hailed with acclamation an arrival that was associated in their minds with steaming bowls of punch. Mrs. Mapp attended her victim up the creaking staircase; for gold and silver tissues are no fitting robes for denizens of spunging-houses, much to the annoyance of the keeperess, whose eyes brightened at sight of what she chose to deem her perquisites.

Madam Mapp talked glibly as she undressed poor Barbara. She must not fret. 'Twas a cunning but permissible stratagem of war. She would go herself to Cleveland Row for garments. Her little maid should bring them in a trice. Her ladyship must not bear malice, for poor folks must live. Nay; the present sojourn should be no longer than the former one. These diamonds would pawn for a goodly sum. She would see about the matter for her patroness, since for the present she was obdurate about the Tripoline. The little maid along with clothes should also bring release.

Thus cackling, Mother Mapp departed on her errand, and Barbara sat silent and unheeding, without effort to collect her thoughts.

It was evening when the fresh blow fell which by

sure presentiment Mrs. Philpot knew was coming. The abigail arrived with more suitable clothes, and was full of lamentation. The Fates were bent on crushing her unhappy mistress. Mother Mapp was a base, bad woman. In some one's pay, no doubt, or she could not be so wicked.

She, the little maid, obeying the instructions of her incarcerated lady, had sold the diamond necklace for what in a hurry it would fetch, and had paid the five hundred guineas. But, as it seemed, the frippery-woman had been playing dark. Her own account was paid; but she yet held others, having bought up several claims which had seemed no better than bad debts. Hence her hapless mistress was not free. Had she, the abigail, known of it, she would have stood out a day or two and have made a better bargain over the brilliants.

Bab sat on the bed and listened, with twined fingers, motionless. The Fates indeed were bent on crushing her.

'Sold the diamonds!' she echoed hoarsely. 'Sold them! Miserable wench! they were not mine to sell. Mother Mapp said something about pawning them—which indeed was wrong. Ah me! what matters it, since now I am quite undone?'

Barbara sat on the bed-edge, petrified; the little maid upon the floor, weeping bitterly. Presently the latter, seeing her mistress so aghast, gave vent to the long, low moan of a wounded beast in the bracken, disconcerting thereby the captains below, who loved hilarity, and who were moodily inclined, sniffing no smell of punch.

'Ah, woe! Ah, woe!' she wailed; 'what have I done?—what have I done?'

'What hast thou done, indeed! oh, only friend that I have left!' responded Barbara grimly; 'what hast thou done, indeed!'

Evening darkened into night while the helpless twain sat eying one another. The telltale square, with its gridiron of bars, no longer offended the sight, being blurred in the pervading gloom. What noise was that, and shuffle of feet? Sure, history was not about to repeat itself after so short an interval in every minute particular? Was the naughty little reprobate, with pallid, dissipated visage, again to come to the rescue?

Barbara caught herself almost hoping so, but chid the thought while yet half-formed. The weeping little maid cheered up, and sprang chirping to her feet.

'How silly a wench am I!' she cried, 'to have forgotten! I met him, and he asked tenderly after your ladyship, and I told him all, and he whistled. He is good, if uncouth and ugly.'

Barbara's brow blackened. She too! Bought by the Tripoline! Was it indeed determined by those Parcæ that she was to be the heroine of Mr. Hogarth's tragedy? If they only would announce at once that it must be, and make an end on't—but what said the little maid, in her rippling, witless prattle?

'Mr. Theophilus! Theo! husband of that other abominable woman! Theo! Much help would he be, seeing that he himself was ever out at elbows, and much dependent on his father.'

And yet—'twas notorious that, like many another, he disliked his wife above all women; and the story of the blind leading the blind oft hath a different ending, for, knowing well the ditch, they learn to keep each other out of it.

Who more experienced than Theo in treading the shifty quicksands? 'Twas with such a welcome as astonished Honest Pistol that Bab sprang up when the door opened, extending both her hands eagerly, yet with no gladness on her face.

'I am in sore trouble, and you will help me?' was all her greeting, as, waving with queenly gesture towards the dusky bed, which bore manifold traces of many occupants, she motioned him to sit.

Theo chuckled and obeyed. Verily he was familiar with many a device, and hearkened, whistling low, his squinting eyes focussed on the tallow dip, wherewith the chirping and now cheerful abigail lighted the conference.

'There are many hands employed over this broth,' he said, when Bab had finished. 'Whose hands and for what object you must determine. This much is plain: you are in a desperate pickle; for those who planned the clever scheme about the diamonds will set the jeweller to prosecute you on a grave charge. You have no cash, and therefore can't dwell here or stop his mouth. Better far at once to accept the prison before the jeweller comes forward. In any case, your protector dead, you must languish somewhere until term. If you take my advice, and in such affairs you can scarce have better—ahem—you will surrender to-morrow at the King's Bench, in the matter of Mother Mapp, and get your name enrolled, while I see about the Rules.'

All this was Greek to Bab; so Theo condescended to explain. Once caged, it signified not how many were the charges, and 'twas always well that a light one should stand first. The spunging-house was invented as a species of Purgatory 'twixt freedom and permanent duress, which the more experienced knew to be in many a case worse than the latter evil. In the spunging-house you were, in sooth, a sponge, to be wrung and wrung with deft swiftness until quite dry. In the prison there were many ways of living like a fighting-cock—of postponing trial, and dwelling comfortably on your income, which, till judgment, might not be touched by creditors.

Thus many debtors abode in comfort for years in the precincts of the King's Bench, by crafty well-tried devices postponing trial, snapping fingers at claimants who gnashed their teeth in vain.

Nor did imprisonment mean of necessity a cage

built of four walls. The Rules were purchasable, by any who could give to the Marshal substantial security, at the rate of ten guineas for the first hundred pounds of the debt, and five pounds for every hundred after.

The Rules of the King's Bench (we have seen that Southwark was on various accounts a labyrinth of 'Liberties') extended over the whole of St. George's Fields, including Blackman Street and a portion of the Borough, embracing a circuit of three miles around the prison; and within this limit those who enjoyed the Rules could live according to their purses. Should it be necessary for a prisoner for any reason to overstep the limit, it was possible three times in a term to procure *day-rules*, whereby the purchaser was free to go where he listed at the cost of 4s. 2d. for the first day, and 3s. 10d. for the following one.

Now, whereas the hereditary Marshal made up his average of eight thousand pounds per annum out of mazy fees and emoluments, out of which he had to pay a warden and turnkeys, and keep all premises in repair, it stood to reason that, when made worth his while, his memory was short anent the number of day-rules paid for. And so it came about (which may puzzle people in a later age, if these things should come to be changed) that many, actresses and actors especially, were able, although prisoners, to carry on their professions on the other side of the river, wandering at will during the daytime, returning to durance at night.

To one so canny as Theo, it seemed, indeed, ridiculous to linger for a minute in a spunging-house when, on demand, you could be transported to so comfortable and convenient an abiding-place for those who are not destitute as the precincts of his Majesty's jails. And such a choice as there was, too!

'In earlier days,' Theo concluded, smirking, 'you used to fancy Southwark for mere amusement; sure 'twill not be so harassing a fate to dwell there in real earnest! Each asylum,' he went on, 'has its advantages and disadvantages, which it behoves a new candidate for admission to weigh carefully.'

Colley's graceless offspring proceeded to reckon up details with a mastery which would have profoundly humiliated his papa.

'The Marshalsea you've seen yourself,' he said. 'The King's Bench hath a pleasing yard, forty yards by eighty, containing a parade nicely paved for promenade; courts for fives and rackets (not much use to a lady); a chapel in the centre, which, indeed, is left to the spiders. Ranged under the lofty outer walls are convenient shops—a trifle dear, no doubt —where butchers, and bakers, and chandlers, and fishmongers ply their several trades. But for the thirty feet of wall and *chevaux de frise* on top, you might suppose yourself in a public market, animated and made gay by the joyous laughter of the players. Then there's the Borough Compter in Tooley Street — small, and in bad repair. The White Lion Bridewell, next St. George's Church. Hum! Dismal —for the folks that hang look in at your window, so close is the gibbet on St. Margaret's Hill. The Clink! Yes. The Clink is the place for Mrs. Philpot,' Theo decided, slapping his thigh with conviction. 'Open and airy towards St. George's Fields. Delightful views over the Thames towards the Tower. Hard by the Bearpit, within easy access of the Dog and Duck and Cooper's Gardens. Certainly the Clink! I'll see about it to-morrow.'

Mr. Cibber was so hearty and apparently well-satisfied, that the guileless abigail clapped her hands in glee, marvelling why everybody didn't rush to engage lodgings in such a charming place. Cleveland Row, albeit under the august shadow of a palace, had been woundily dull. Bearpit! Cooper's Gardens! Dog and Duck! Delicious! Turning to her mistress, she was amazed to perceive that her gloom remained unlightened. Barbara knew the Southwark jails only too well; had she not visited them? Live on your income! Yes; but what if you have none? The common side—home of carking care and dire misery, and cold and slow starvation! Well! for her the avenue with the grave at the end of it would not prove a very long one.

Theo was right in this much. Better to accept

the forbidding inevitable, and clasp it to one's heart to freeze there, than toy with it at a distance. This time there were no guineas in her purse—so much the better. She would place herself in Theo's hands, and leave the spunging-house to-morrow.

END OF VOL. II.

www.ingramcontent.com/pod-product-compliance
Lightning Source LLC
Chambersburg PA
CBHW022020240426
43667CB00042B/1008